EVERY DAY A MIRACLE

EVERY DAY A MIRACLE

TRUSTING THE GOD WHO HEALS US INSIDE AND OUT

MATTHEW STEPHEN BROWN

W PUBLISHING GROUP

AN IMPRINT OF THOMAS NELSON

Published in Nashville, Tennessee, by W Publishing, an imprint of Thomas Nelson.

Thomas Nelson titles may be purchased in bulk for educational, business, fundraising, or sales promotional use. For information, please email SpecialMarkets@ThomasNelson.com.

Unless otherwise noted, Scripture quotations are taken from the ESV® Bible (The Holy Bible, English Standard Version®). ESV® Text Edition: 2016. Copyright © 2001 by Crossway, a publishing ministry of Good News Publishers. The ESV® text has been reproduced in cooperation with and by permission of Good News Publishers. Unauthorized reproduction of this publication is prohibited. All rights reserved.

Scripture quotations marked NIV are taken from the Holy Bible, New International Version®, NIV®. Copyright © 1973, 1978, 1984, 2011 by Biblica, Inc.® Used by permission of Zondervan. All rights reserved worldwide. www.zondervan.com. The "NIV" and "New International Version" are trademarks registered in the United States Patent and Trademark Office by Biblica, Inc.®

Scripture quotations marked NLT are taken from the Holy Bible, New Living Translation. Copyright © 1996, 2004, 2015 by Tyndale House Foundation. Used by permission of Tyndale House Ministries, Carol Stream, Illinois 60188. All rights reserved.

Italics added to Scripture quotations are the author's emphasis.

Some names and identifying details have been changed to protect the privacy of the individuals involved.

The information in this book has been carefully researched by the author and is intended to be a source of information only. The author and the publisher assume no responsibility for any injuries suffered or damages or losses incurred during or as a result of the use or application of the information contained herein.

Any internet addresses, phone numbers, or company or product information printed in this book are offered as a resource and are not intended in any way to be or to imply an endorsement by Thomas Nelson, nor does Thomas Nelson vouch for the existence, content, or services of these sites, phone numbers, companies, or products beyond the life of this book.

ISBN 978-0-7852-4084-6 (audiobook)
ISBN 978-0-7852-4083-9 (ePub)
ISBN 978-0-7852-4082-2 (softcover)

Library of Congress Control Number: 2023941249

Printed in the United States of America
23 24 25 26 27 LBC 5 4 3 2 1

This book is dedicated to all the courageous people who have allowed me to share their stories so that you, the reader, could be reminded that Jesus is still working and doing miracles to bring about the healing that is so needed in your life, drawing you into a deeper, more authentic relationship with Him.

CONTENTS

INTRODUCTION

JESUS OUR HEALER

The last few years have been exhausting. We all have had enough division, devastation, and disease to last us a lifetime. March 2020 changed the world forever, and no matter what I say about the pandemic, I would lose almost half my readers. COVID-19 has negatively affected politics, sports, media, and even many churches. Many Christians now have more faith in conspiracy theories than in Christ.

As a pastor, I struggled during the pandemic to find a way to bring people's focus back to the church's mission—to be real with themselves, God, and others. I sensed God was working, but no matter how I tried to turn our congregation's attention toward the light of what Christ was doing around us, all they could see was the darkness around them. I lost friends, some family members stopped speaking to me, and I saw my church shrink almost by half. I preached about everything I could think of, but nothing I did seemed to help. We were losing people, and people seemed to be losing faith.

Beginning in 2020, the country moved from one issue to the next: COVID-19, the death of George Floyd, riots, and the January 6 storming of the US Capitol. Then Putin got bored and invaded Ukraine. And let's not forget the earth-quakes, murder hornets, and how things got so crazy the potential discovery of aliens was back-page news! I had done everything possible to help our congregation yet had never felt so ill-equipped for leadership. I came to the end of myself as a leader. I didn't know what to do, and I didn't know where to turn.

Like many leaders, I didn't have the answers. I thought the world had changed and flown right by me. I thought I was too old and irrelevant, and for the first time in a long time I considered doing something else for a living. Many people around me were quitting their jobs and moving to other states, and I thought that was what I was supposed to do too. But I prayed about it and heard a clear no. So many Christians were fleeing California, but I felt convicted to stay. As I prayed, I realized I was not supposed to leave.

God impressed upon me that things had not changed but rather the truth was finally being revealed. Those years had not changed us but *exposed* us! They caused us to question whether most Christians were more political than spiritual and more fearful than faithful. COVID did not create cracks in our country, family, or faith; it just made the cracks so large we could no longer ignore them. The pandemic revealed that we are all broken people. Our world is broken, our political system is broken, and our churches are broken.

The more I pressed on, the more I began to see that the world needed healing. The Holy Spirit began to work in me and speak powerfully to me, revealing that I had spent those few years focusing on the problem, not the solution. The more I thought about this idea, the more I saw confirmation that I needed to stop preaching about disaster, disease, and division.

Then I heard a word from Jesus—one word. A real word, a powerful word. *Healer.*

The word *healer* captivated me. No matter what, I couldn't get that word out of my head. Everywhere I turned, I felt the Holy Spirit press upon me to speak on healing. I had never done a healing service before, much less a healing sermon series. I was nervous, but I knew this was what God wanted me to do.

So I changed my sermon calendar, and then I saw Jesus change my church. Over the years I have seen God do miracles, but nothing like what I saw God do during our series on healing.

In this book I share some of the biblical truths I explored in that series. At the end of each chapter I have included three features:

1. A prayer to draw you closer to God, especially when praying for a miracle, and to help you utilize some of the tools mentioned in that chapter.
2. A QR code to a short video of me speaking on that chapter's topic to help you on your journey of praying for miracles every day!
3. Discussion questions, which I highly encourage you

to reflect on with a friend or in a small group, to help you wrestle through your hopes, doubts, and fears.

So many Christians know Jesus as Savior, but so few have come to know Him as Healer. The Scriptures reveal that Jesus is our Lord and that Jesus is our Savior. But the Bible reveals that Jesus is also our Healer. Do you know Him as Healer?

ONE

KNOWING ALL OF JESUS

─────────────

JESUS SAID TO HIM, "HAVE I BEEN WITH YOU SO LONG, AND YOU STILL DO NOT KNOW ME?"
JOHN 14:9

Every day there is an opportunity for a miracle, and at some point, you will find yourself in need of one. One ordinary day, I was in a grocery store in the bread aisle. I remember exactly where I was because I am strictly gluten-free. I love the smell of bread, but bread does not love me! A woman came up to me. "Are you Matt Brown?" Yes, I said. "Pastor Matt Brown?" Again I said yes. "I'm so sorry to interrupt your shopping. I'm so sorry to bother you—" And then she started crying almost uncontrollably.

It took the woman a few moments to pull herself to-gether enough to speak, and at first I couldn't understand what she was trying to say through her tears. She took a much-needed deep breath. "It's my marriage. We have two little kids—" She started crying again. And then she said, "I need prayer, Pastor Matt. We need prayer. We need a miracle, or we are not going to make it." I did not know her, but I knew what she needed. It's what we all need when we need a miracle. We need Jesus!

Right there in the grocery store, with people doing their best to avoid the scene, I asked her if I could pray for her. "Yes, yes," she said, "please!" And I prayed to Jesus with a stranger for a miracle for her marriage.

When you need a miracle, where will you go?

Some people reach for science, and we certainly have seen miraculous scientific breakthroughs in our lifetimes. Other people reach for healthy lifestyle changes. They start diets, get serious about exercise, and swear off vices. Some of us pursue meditation, and others dive deep into coun-seling. These things aren't bad in and of themselves. As a matter of fact, many people find the help they need from these things. But where do we go when nothing works and everything we have tried has failed?

Sadly, God is often not our first choice. Even people who claim God is first in everything seem to turn to Him last when they need a miracle. Why is it that, for so many of us who consider ourselves Christians, Jesus is often the afterthought when our life or someone else's is on the line? Many Christians are religious when it comes to everyday life but practically atheists when it comes to miracles they need every day.

When we read about Jesus in the Bible, He seems so different from the Jesus we experience daily. What have we forgotten or failed to discover about Jesus that His early followers knew? Even those who rejected Jesus as the Messiah accepted the fact that He performed miracles. His messiahship was in question; His miracles were not! Many of today's believers are exactly the opposite. We accept Him as our Savior but reject Him as our miraculous Healer. We need to rediscover Him as both.

THE SON OF MAN FORGIVES AND HEALS

In Mark 2, the heading in many Bibles reads something like this: "The Son of Man Forgives and Heals." The church still proclaims this first part, but sadly many have forgotten the second part.

Jesus was in a house in Capernaum, preaching and teaching as He often did. His teaching and His presence drew incredible crowds. More people wanted to see Jesus than the house could hold. Among this crowd were four men with a friend who was paralyzed.

We don't know for sure, but I imagine these men had tried everything to help their friend, and nothing had worked. Consider what people are willing to do nowadays when they need to be healed. In some cases, they will travel the globe seeking miracle cures and miraculous healers. Some people are so desperate they will spend every last dime seeking the healing they need. These four friends may not have spent all their money, but they were willing to give all their strength to get their friend to Jesus. Why? Because everyone knew Jesus could heal. Jesus was known in His country as Healer before He was ever known to the world as Savior.

The four friends wanted to see Jesus, but the crowd was too large, and there was no way to get this paralyzed man through the front door. But the friends didn't quit; they improvised. These four friends knew something about Jesus we may have forgotten: Jesus can do miracles no matter how bad or bleak the situation. So they figured out how to get their paralyzed friend on the roof, cut a hole in the roof, and lowered their friend on his makeshift stretcher to the feet of Jesus.

> Jesus can do miracles no matter how bad or bleak the situation.

Seeing the faith of these friends, Jesus forgave the paralyzed man of his spiritual sins. He said, "Son, your sins are forgiven" (Mark 2:5). This must have been some spectacle—vandalism, interruption, and then confusion.

I imagine that to these four friends, Jesus seemed to have missed the entire point of all the work they had done. In their limited understanding, they likely believed Jesus healed their friend's soul but ignored his obvious need for a physical miracle. But it wasn't Jesus who missed the point; it was almost everyone else.

The house was filled with religious people who thought, *This Jesus is ridiculous! Only God can forgive sins.* They also considered His words claiming to forgive sins to be blasphemy, which in the Jewish faith practiced two thousand years ago was a crime that carried the death penalty. Jesus knew what these religious people were thinking, so He asked, "Why do you question these things in your hearts? Which is easier, to say to the paralytic, 'Your sins are forgiven,' or to say, 'Rise, take up your bed and walk'?" (vv. 8–9).

This is a question that still stands today. Which is easier: To heal or to save? Many people can heal, but only one Person can save.

Jesus didn't want His audience to feel bad; He wanted them to know God. So He continued, "'But that you may know that the Son of Man has authority on earth to forgive sins . . . I say to you, rise, pick up your bed, and go home'" (vv. 10–11).

Jesus knows how hard it is for you and me to trust Him. We struggle every day to believe in Him. So He patiently reveals Himself even to His harshest critics. Jesus wants you and me to know He can heal and save.

The paralyzed man was healed instantly. He picked up his mat and walked out on his own two feet. It took four friends to get him there but only a word from Jesus for him to leave on his own. He was completely healed! Everyone was astounded. The four friends, the audience, the critics, and even the formerly paralyzed man all gave glory to God and said, "We never saw anything like this!" (v. 12).

Have you ever seen anything like that? This kind of healing didn't happen on just one or two occasions but almost everywhere Jesus went. Wherever people found Jesus, they found healing. Jesus performed this miracle so that we may know something about the Son of Man—which is Jesus' favorite term for Himself. (We find this term over eighty times in the Gospels; most of them are quotes from Jesus referring to Himself.) He wants us to know that He came both to heal and save. You may know Jesus as your Savior, but do you know Him as your Healer?

BARRIERS TO KNOWING JESUS AS HEALER

One of the most significant barriers to people genuinely knowing Jesus as Healer is the fear of admitting they don't know Him in that way. *They know how to be religious but don't know anything about the healing Jesus.*

I had the privilege of being raised by parents who taught me about Jesus. As a pastor, I'm lucky if I can get people to come to church once a month. As a kid, I went to church three times a week! But even after all that time at church, I knew little about Jesus the Healer. So in my early twenties, when I had finally perfected stupidity, I decided to leave my life of foolishness and really give Jesus a try. One of the things that blew me away when I started to read the Bible for myself was discovering how many miracles Jesus performed.

In our Bibles, we have four accounts of Jesus' life: Matthew, Mark, Luke, and John. These four gospels record thirty-seven miracles. Thirty-seven! These miracles are meant not only to help us know the power of Jesus but also to know something more about Jesus. Of the thirty-seven miracles recorded in the Bible, twenty-eight were healing miracles. Jesus wanted to be known as a miracle worker who could heal, and He wants to be known by you and by me in this way. No matter what you have done and where you are, Jesus is in the business of revealing Himself to people who do not truly know Him in a miraculous way.

> **No matter what you have done and where you are, Jesus is in the business of revealing Himself to people who do not truly know Him in a miraculous way.**

Paul's Miraculous Encounter with Jesus

One of the most transformed people in the history of the world was the apostle Paul. He wasn't just an idiot in his twenties; he was also violent! He went from hating Jesus and hunting Christians to loving Jesus and leading Christians. What made Paul so different during his ministry was that he didn't just believe in Jesus; *he knew the miraculous Jesus!* The *moment* Paul met the living Jesus, he was transformed from a hater of Jesus to His devoted follower. What changed Paul's life was a miraculous encounter with Him. Paul went from total ignorance to total transformation.

While he was on the road to the Middle Eastern city of Damascus to arrest Christians, Paul was struck with a blinding light and heard a voice from heaven saying, "Why are you persecuting me?" Paul, known then as Saul, said, "Who are you, lord?" The voice replied, "I am Jesus" (Acts 9:3–5 NLT). Paul met Jesus and was changed—in a moment. Paul used to think that a once-dead-but-now-living Jesus was ridiculous. But the resurrection became a miraculous reality when the Lord Jesus opened his eyes.

This same living Jesus can change you if you are willing to open yourself up to a new experience with Him. Jesus died but miraculously came back to life. He can do miracles in your life. But for that to happen, you, like Paul, need a new experience with Him.

God was not done with Paul, and God is not done with you. After Paul met the living Jesus, Paul could no longer see. He was blind. Paul had been enlightened by Jesus but was desperate for a healing miracle from Him. He prayed and fasted for three days (vv. 9, 11). God had not left Paul but was teaching Paul something every believer needs to know: Jesus is not only God above but a Healer here below! Jesus instructed a reluctant believer named Ananias to place his hands on Paul and say, "'Brother Saul, the Lord Jesus, who appeared to you on the road, has sent me so that you might regain your sight and be filled with the Holy Spirit.' Instantly, something like scales fell from Saul's eyes, and he regained his sight" (vv. 17–18 NLT).

Paul had to meet the living Jesus to be saved, but he had to be healed through Ananias to be sent. Jesus wants both to save you and to send you.

Miracles Draw in Those Who Are Far from God

Our world is moving away from the Christian faith. Thousands of young people list their religious affiliation as "none," so they are called the Nones. They believe in nothing. Real miracles can help move them from nothing to at least considering there might be something. Miracles are real-life examples of the reality of God. This is why Jesus performed miracles for others long before He died on the cross.

We live in a day and age where we think we have an answer for everything. Miracles don't provide answers; they demand we ask bigger questions. Many people rejected Jesus when He was on earth, but His miracles forced people at least to consider Him. Many people today won't even consider Jesus. They have absolutely no desire to know Him. To them, He is just another religious figure who has no real effect on their lives. Religion pushes people away from God, but miracles can draw them in.

> Miracles don't provide answers; they demand we ask bigger questions.

Jesus used miracles amid a wicked and corrupt generation to make them take a look. That's why wherever Jesus went, huge crowds followed. They wanted to experience a miracle that would make a difference in their lives. People followed after Jesus not only because they heard He could save them but because they heard He could feed them. As religious people, we are often concerned about empty buildings when others are concerned about empty bellies. Many people don't have time for faith because they struggle with life.

I have a friend who is not religious. He would be considered a None. I wasn't exactly sure what he believed about God, but I knew what he thought about religion. He thought religion was a scam or a crutch for weak-willed people. He was never going to come to my church, no matter how clever my sermon series was or how convenient we made it for him. No matter how many times I invited him, he wasn't interested. Growing up, he had some horrible experiences with religious Christians. His wounds robbed him of his faith and gave him a deep sense of mistrust for religion. He was not a bad guy; he just had zero interest in becoming a follower of Jesus. His life was full, and in his mind, he was happy. He didn't need God.

Then he got really sick.

The hospital was confused as to how to treat him. He had some unusual form of pneumonia that didn't respond to antibiotics. No matter what the doctors tried, he got worse. Eventually, he was moved to the intensive care unit of the hospital. His oxygen levels plummeted, and the hospital staff scrambled to stabilize him. It didn't make any sense; he should have been getting better. The ICU staff told him if his oxygen levels crashed again, he would have to be placed in a medically induced coma.

He was justifiably terrified. He asked the nurse to set up a FaceTime with me. I could barely hear him speak over the large tube pumping air into his nose. He said he was at the maximum oxygen level they could pump without damaging his lungs. Anytime he moved, his body's demand for oxygen would exceed his ability to take it in. I asked him if he wanted me to pray for him and ask God to give him a miracle. My unbelieving, skeptical friend said yes, he would! At this point in his illness, he *needed* a miracle. The whole time I had known him, he had never come to church or opened a Bible. But due to a near-death experience in the

ICU, he opened up his heart to the remote chance that the God he was not even sure existed would do a miracle.

> **Miracles show the world that God is real and that He can make a difference.**

I prayed for him over FaceTime as long as the nurse let me. My friend did not get put into a coma. He went home two days later, completely healed. What medicine could not do, Jesus did. He opened my friend's heart ever so slightly to God, and God opened up His power to him. Miracles show the world that God is real and that He can make a difference.

Miracles Encourage Those Who Love God

Miracles don't just draw in people far from God; they encourage those who love God and are devoted to Him. Miracles pump us up and encourage our faith. They remind us that God hears us when we pray.

This book is a highlight reel of some of the most powerful miracles I have seen during my years of ministry as a pastor. Some of the miracles in this book are so profound they will be hard for you to believe. I would have struggled to believe them if I had not been there myself.

Like in the Bible, these miracles are about real people with real issues. When I have their permission, I will use their real names and give you as many details as possible to help you on your faith journey. In some cases, the people's names have been changed to protect their privacy. But all these stories are true.

You will read about God hearing the cries of His people

and dramatically answering their prayers. You will read about powerful miracles and deliverances. In our final chapter, you will read about God bringing someone back from the dead—in front of my eyes.

We are in the last days, my friend. God has not left us but is doing something powerful again. He is moving in the world to draw people back to Himself. As you read through these chapters, you will be challenged to believe in what Jesus can do. You will be taught to ask for what you need Him to do, you will learn how to wait on God's answer, and you will be encouraged to accept His answer no matter what it is.

But for you and me to experience the miraculous power of Jesus and truly know Him for all He is, we must open ourselves up to a new experience with Jesus.

A NEW EXPERIENCE WITH JESUS

New experiences can be scary. On my first day of seminary, my pastor gave me some well-meaning but terrible advice. He said, "If it's something new, it's not for you." It rhymes, but it is wrong. He didn't want seminary to change me with radical ideas. But I needed to be changed. I needed something new, and so many people who sit in church week after week feel the same. You and I will continually need new experiences with Jesus to get to know Him better. That's why heaven is forever: because it will take an eternity to unpack all that Jesus truly is.

Throughout the two-thousand-year history of Christianity, our understanding of Jesus has been hotly debated. What we emphasize about Jesus has changed. Even though the Jesus we worship as Christians is the same, what we focus on about Him is often different. The good news is, no matter how many denominations or understandings of Jesus there may be, the Bible presents only the one Jesus who *is*. The author of the book of Hebrews stated it this way: "Jesus Christ is the same yesterday and today and forever" (13:8). That's why we are so blessed to have Scripture. Regardless of our opinions and religious backgrounds, the real Jesus is preserved within the Scriptures. Jesus doesn't change, but everything else does.

The same Jesus who did thirty-seven miracles in Scripture is the same Jesus who can and will do miracles in the lives of those who ask!

The world is changing faster than ever. I hardly recognize it as the world I grew up in. So many of my fellow Christians think we are here to change the world. I don't see it that way. I can't think of a more pointless thing to try to do. Part of the reason the world is such a mess is that we are constantly trying to change everyone else.

This book is not about changing the world. The world is doing that on its own. This book is about inviting its readers to the one thing that *doesn't* change in this world: the one constant, unchanging, eternal force. Times change, the weather changes, and we change. That's why we have so much confusion about Jesus. The Bible tells us that Jesus never changes and warns us not to be led away by any new version of Him. But that's what we do. We are led away by a strange new Jesus, or we are in love with the very old version from our religious tradition—one that was once a strange new Jesus but has now been around so long we think it's the original Jesus.

DO YOU KNOW THE MIRACULOUS JESUS?

So do you know the miraculous Jesus? Many Christians think they know Him but are afraid to ask Him for what they need. Once you know Him for who He is, you will never fear asking for what you think you need! You will not be afraid of praying, and you will run to Jesus with your requests because knowing Jesus changes everything. It changes the way you look at life and the way you pray in the face of death.

To experience this kind of miracle, you must know Jesus for who He is. Jesus did not want to be loved for what He could *do* but because of who He *was*. He is the Miracle Worker. But before He changes your health, marriage, finances, or any area of your life, He must first change your mind!

To meet the real Jesus, we must be willing to meet Him for who He is. In C. S. Lewis's allegory *The Screwtape Letters*, the fictional demon Screwtape warns his nephew Wormwood of the most dangerous prayer by a believer: "For if he ever comes to make the distinction, if ever he consciously directs his prayers 'Not to what I think thou art but to what thou knowest thyself to be.'" I have memorized the thought this way—the most dangerous prayer is not to who you think God is, but to who He knows Himself to be. This kind of prayer will not change who God is, but it will change who you think God is. This prayer allows you to remove the self-created barriers that keep you from knowing God more deeply.

You may be a scholar, a lifelong church member, or a pastor. You could be a skeptic or just confused. I humbly ask that you consider that you may have missed an essential part of who Jesus is and what He came to do. If you are willing to reconsider how you see Jesus, I believe it will change your life and the lives of those you love. You will fall deeply in love with Jesus and find a true desire to share with everyone you meet all that Jesus is and has done for you.

The world needs to know that Jesus is more than just a Savior. He is also our Healer. When the world begins to experience how Jesus can heal, it will be more interested in how He can save. That's why, when the paralyzed man was brought before the feet of Jesus, Jesus both saved and healed him!

Unfortunately, some people who believe in Jesus as Savior no longer believe in Him as Healer. They have given up hope for healing because of their personal experience or what they have been taught. This does not have to be your story. It can change with a simple but powerful prayer. Ask Jesus to show you who He is and what He wants to do. Don't demand; ask. Stop reading, put down the book, and pray, "Jesus, show me who You are!"

Stop and pray that now—the book can wait, but your heart can't.

The good news is, if you pray that prayer, Jesus will answer it. He has been answering it for nearly two thousand years. Even in His day, when the powerful and the political missed Him, the desperate and diseased found Him. Are you desperate? Are you battling disease? Are you ready to stop playing religious games? Then you need to know about another side of Jesus.

FOLLOWING JESUS IN THE STORM

If you are ready to know more about Jesus, then you need to know that some things about Jesus can't be gleaned from a book. You can only learn them in a sinking boat. The greatest Christian song of all time, in my opinion, is "It Is Well with My Soul." The lyrics were written by Horatio Spafford more than one hundred years ago. Most people have forgotten his story, but his song remains and still blesses people. He did not write this song after a church service, an in-depth Bible study, or after a vision from God. He wrote it after a terrible boat accident that took the lives of his children.

I would never wish what happened to him on anyone. I have held parents who have lost a child. It was awful! Spafford lost all his children. He wrote the words while looking upon the spot where his four daughters had recently died after their boat sank. He lost them all in life but found a healing Jesus in his grief.

Your greatest moments with God will come from your

greatest suffering in life. To know Jesus as Healer, you have to trust Him in your pain. You must invite Jesus into your storm just as Jesus invited the disciples into His. We will discuss this storm on the Sea of Galilee in detail in the next chapter. The storm is not where you or I ever want to be, but that's where our knowledge of Jesus truly grows, and that's why He invites us out into the storm. He invites us into what we fear so we can find what we need.

> **Your greatest moments with God will come from your greatest suffering in life.**

Just as Jesus would call the disciples to cross the lake at night, He allows us to leave the safety of what we know so we can truly experience what we don't know—and what we don't know is all of Him. If we can find the courage to paddle out with Jesus into the sea, we'll do so at the risk of our lives. But if we stay on the shore, choosing comfort over calling, we'll risk our souls. Your instinct will tell you to stay where you are. Your soul will tell you to go where Jesus is. Your tradition and current understanding will challenge you to stay with what you know. Jesus will call you into the current to reveal what you don't yet know. Jesus calls us to love Him as He has loved us. True love demands depth, and depth is found in the storm.

This book will call you to paddle out regardless of your pain because there are characteristics of Jesus that can be seen only through tears. Spafford discovered that it was well with his soul only after his soul was crushed. I am sorry for your tears—don't waste them; they are precious. I am so sorry for your pain, but you don't have to stay where you are. Jesus, the Healer, is calling you from where you are to where He knows you can be. He is calling you from what you are to what He made you to be. But to become all God has made you to be, you must choose to become it.

You and I are defined not by our surroundings but by our choices. You must choose to follow Jesus. He calls but never coerces. He invites you to get in the boat, but He will not force you to. You can live your life on the shore or trust Him in the boat. What will you do? I know the shore is comfortable and the sea is scary. You are used to the warmth and comfort of the sand, but you cannot grow past where you are. To grow, you must move and paddle out to get to the boat. Jesus won't paddle for you. He died for you, but He won't paddle for you. The cross was His work; the paddle out is yours.

All twelve disciples were confronted with this same choice: choose the ordinary life you know, or choose an extraordinary life by following the Jesus you don't yet fully know. The twelve disciples had a choice, and so do you: stay where you are, or follow Jesus into the boat. The day was over, but their journey had just begun. Your story is not over; it is just beginning. There is a reason for your suffering and your storm. Regardless of the outcome, you will meet the One whom even the winds and waves obey!

THE MIRACLE YOU NEED

I cannot promise you will get the miracle you want, but I can promise you will receive the miracle you *need*. I hope the chapters in this book will become pages in your own story—where Jesus lifts you from where you are, to where you need to be, to where you are *called* to be. No matter where you are with Jesus, there is always more to know and experience.

Jesus is miraculous! He can and does still heal. Healing is not something we need only when we receive bad news, are diagnosed with a disease, or are in a terrible accident. The miracle of healing is something we need every day and every week of every year. This book will take you on a journey of learning to trust the God who heals from the inside out!

The first miracle you need is to learn how to see God's presence in your pain.

PRAY

Lord Jesus, help me to step out of my comfort zone and willingly learn more about You. I want to know all that You would have me know. Open my heart and enlighten my mind to the truth that You are both my Savior and my Healer. I pray this in Your name, amen.

WATCH

REFLECT

1. Describe a time in your life when you learned something new about Jesus that you hadn't known before but wished you had.
2. Why do you think we might be closed-minded to new experiences with Jesus?
3. How could seeing Jesus as Savior *and* Healer help you share the hope you have with others?
4. Where might you need to grow in your understanding of Jesus as Healer as you read this book?

TWO

THE MIRACLE OF GOD'S PRESENCE

"BEHOLD, I AM WITH YOU ALWAYS."
MATTHEW 28:20

W hen life is no longer what we thought, one of the first things we discover is who is with us. There are people who say they will be there for us but are nowhere to be found when we need them the most. I had a guy in my church who told me he would always be by my side. He said he was built for it. I could count on him! He said that no matter what happened, he would be there. He said he would take a bullet for me. I last saw him almost twenty years ago. What happened? Life happened, and I never fired even one shot!

We discover who someone truly is in the storms of life. Some friends will stand with you over a cup of coffee, but other friends will stand with you over a coffin. Genuine relationships are not formed at the beach; they are formed in a storm. We all need more than fair-weather friends. We need people who will celebrate with us, hold us, pray for us, serve us, and clean us up if necessary. It is during tragedies that we discover who the genuine friends in our lives really are.

Years ago, I met a man who was hit by a car. He had pulled over to help someone on the freeway whose car had a flat tire. A drunk driver, drawn to the flashing hazard lights on the side of the road, ran into my friend. That night, this man risked it all to be a good Samaritan. Instantly, he lost his health, he lost his job, and he almost lost his marriage. But the Jesus he met in his storm was not the Jesus he thought he knew.

He met the Jesus who comforted his soul and healed his body and every aspect of his life. This is the Jesus we must meet in the storm because there is more to Jesus than you and I know.

THE JESUS WE KNOW FROM SCRIPTURE

The Jesus we know from Scripture appeared almost two thousand years ago, and the world has never been the same. The Jesus of history was a Jew from Nazareth, a nowhere town in a mostly forgotten place. Nazareth was a challenged area in the hills of northern Palestine. Most of us were taught that Jesus was a carpenter, but *tektōn*, the Greek word translated as "carpenter," should probably be translated as "stonemason." Jesus was a man who worked with His hands.

There were not a lot of trees in Nazareth, so almost everything in Jesus' time was built with stone. Nazareth was near a rock quarry, so as a man in construction, He most likely worked with stone, not wood. Jesus would have known how to cut, shape, and build with rock. This is probably why He said wise people build their houses on rock (Matthew 7:24).

As a child, Jesus would have learned the craft passed down to Him by His father, Joseph. By the time Jesus started His public ministry around thirty years old, He would have mastered His father's craft. So the twelve disciples could have learned plenty from Him about building with stone, but they would likely not have asked Him anything about water. The *only* thing rocks are suitable for in water is increasing the speed at which you sink! But it is precisely on the water where the disciples were forced to ask the most crucial question about Jesus: "Who then is this, that even the wind and the sea obey him?" (Mark 4:41).

Jesus has the most to teach in the areas of our lives where we think we can learn the least from Him. It is not until we discover our profound weakness in the storms of life that we can experience His true strength from heaven. As the Bible teaches, His power works perfectly with our weakness (2 Corinthians 12:9). When we discover how weak we are, we discover how strong we can be in Him.

But to truly know Jesus, we must start with a big storm on a small lake.

A Big Storm on a Small Lake

This big storm on a small lake is found in three books of the Bible: Matthew (8:23–27), Mark (4:35–41), and Luke (8:22–25). The Bible is full of stories about Jesus—all of them revealing something important about Him. But this story is essential to us and our journey of discovery about Jesus. This story is important because it forced the disciples to question who Jesus really was. Not just the Jesus they *thought* they knew but the Jesus they *needed* to know. This is exactly what we need to do: move from what we think we know about Jesus to what we need to know about Jesus.

As we look at the story of this storm from three different perspectives, we have to ask some serious questions. Why are there three accounts and not just one? Why do the stories differ, and why does John's gospel omit it entirely? These questions lead some people to give up on the Christian faith altogether. They see subtle differences and omissions in Scripture as reasons to stop believing. But these subtle differences help us to know the stories are authentic. A good detective knows that when everyone is telling the exact same story, everyone is most likely lying. Identical stories are usually fabricated; authentic stories leave room for difference.

Years ago, I was an eyewitness to an attempted murder. I had just finished surfing and was headed to my car. I was wet, tired, and covered in sand. I heard people shouting and looked over to see a homeless man and a woman screaming at each other. To my astonishment, the woman pulled an ax from her shopping cart.

The man she yelled at did not take her actions seriously and casually turned to walk away. As he turned, she hit him with the ax. First, she hit him in the back of the arm, and then as he fell to the ground, she hit him in the back. I watched in horror as the ax sank deep into his back. I honestly thought he was dead. To this day, I have never seen anything even remotely as terrifying.

I was in shock. I didn't know what to do, so I started shouting at her to stop—and she did. Then she turned and came at me with the ax. Most of what happened after that is a blur, except for a few random details. This crime occurred in Waikiki Beach, Hawaii, in front of hundreds of eyewitnesses. I was so shaken by the event that when the police arrived on the scene with guns drawn, I didn't realize I had the ax in my hands.

Whenever you go through a traumatic event, the way you remember it is strange. All near-death experiences are similar in that the brain focuses on some details but not all. You have the same big picture as others but the details differ between witnesses.

When I gave my eyewitness testimony to the detectives, much of what had happened was murky in my mind. The police officers were frustrated by the lack of details I could provide. I could not remember simple things like the woman's height, hair color, or ethnicity. The detectives found that hard to believe, but I hadn't focused on her clothing as she charged me. I was looking at the ax!

The detective said, "You can't identify *anything* about

her?" I thought about it, and after about an hour, I remembered something. I told the detective I remembered the color of her underwear! She had turquoise-blue underwear. The detective laughed. He thought I was being funny, but I wasn't joking. He told me he had interviewed dozens of eyewitnesses. "No one, and I mean no one, saw her underwear," he said.

The more I thought about it, the more I remembered the underwear. I told the officer that when she charged me with the ax, I ran toward her instead of running from her as the other man had done. As she raised the ax, I went for it. I grabbed it from her as we tumbled to the ground. Everything went in slow motion like you see in the movies. As we fell to the ground wrestling with the ax, her pants slid down, and I remember seeing her underwear.

The detective said, "Turquoise?"

I said yes.

He called me the next day, laughing. "Turquoise. They were turquoise, just like you said."

It is in the details and slight differences that we find the entire story. Even in the slightest changes in the disciples' stories, we find the authentic Jesus.

Even though the story of this storm differs slightly in three accounts, we need all three angles to get the complete picture. We need this story from three perspectives to see all God wants us to see. Luke gave us this story from the perspective of the investigator—much like the man who interviewed dozens of eyewitnesses in the attempted murder on Waikiki Beach. He was not present for the event but provided the most accurate picture of what happened based on eyewitness accounts. Luke included everything he thought was credible and valuable to our understanding of the miraculous event.

Matthew's and Mark's perspectives on this story were slightly different. They did not use a collection of many eyewitness accounts. Instead, each perspective comes primarily from one eyewitness.

Matthew's account is deeply personal. I think this story scared the heck out of Matthew, and that's why this story was placed in his gospel differently than in Mark's and Luke's. He placed it in his eighth chapter, immediately after talking about counting the cost of following Jesus. Matthew was an accountant; he counted the cost as a profession. This storm caused him to recalculate his life. He counted the cost, and it was immediately after this story that Jesus personally called Matthew to leave everything behind and to follow Him.

In Luke's and Mark's gospels, Matthew was called to follow Jesus before the storm, but Matthew placed the storm *before* his personal calling. Why was Matthew's recollection different? As a Jewish writer, Matthew was not just interested in an accurate chronology of the life of Jesus but in an accurate account of the theology of the person of Jesus. His memory of the moment moved him from an observer of Jesus to a follower of Jesus. Matthew had come to know Jesus as someone worth leaving everything for. Matthew was no fool. He was successful and smart. He wasn't leaving everything for a stranger who said, "Follow me" (Matthew 9:9). He left everything for a Jesus he had *seen* and come to *know*. Matthew wanted us to know that he left everything for the One "even winds and sea obey" (8:27).

Mark's account is probably not all of Mark's own experience. According to some early church leaders, Mark's gospel was heavily influenced by Peter's sermons that he preached in Rome. Mark would have heard these sermons repeatedly and been shaped by them. For Mark, this was the story where his fearless leader, Peter, a brave fisherman, became a coward and cried out for Jesus, the stonemason, to save them. Mark understood this was where Peter faced losing everything. Peter was a natural leader, and as a leader, he had a different level of risk. Not only would Peter have feared for his life and the lives of his friends, but the storm would have resulted in the loss of his family's wealth and future. With him and his boats gone, nothing would be left for his family but absolute ruin.

This was where Peter's eyes were first opened to the reality that there was more to Jesus than he knew.

If this story is crucial to understanding Jesus, why isn't it in John's gospel? The answer is simple—this wasn't a moment that moved or changed the apostle John. It was a moment for John; it just wasn't *his* moment. Different people have different moments with God. You don't need to be in someone else's moment with God. You are in your own story and need your *own* moment. If you haven't had yours yet, I pray that it comes.

> Different people have different moments with God.

This storm was a significant moment for the disciples. It was recorded in three gospels so it could become a major moment for you!

The story of the storm began late one evening. It had been a long day and was dark, and Jesus said, "Let's go sailing." I love the water; I always have. But I have never been a fan of being on or in the water at night. Water is scary enough in the daylight, but it's terrifying at night. Dark water plays tricks on your mind, and dark skies can make it worse. Nowadays, we have lights that can pierce the darkness, navigational equipment that gives our precise location, and distress signals that send an SOS for help and guide our rescuers to where we are. The disciples had none of that. It was dark, and they were tired. Jesus was so tired He took a nap! But they headed out into the darkness. The disciples rowed, and Jesus slept. Jesus slept sounder, and the night got darker and scarier.

Then a storm arose from nowhere—the worst ones always do.

The gospel writers considered this a biblical storm, almost supernatural. If you have ever been on the water during severe weather, you know how quickly things can get out of hand. Overconfidence gets people into the most dangerous situations. At least four of the disciples were experienced fishermen. They had been there before; after all, the Sea of Galilee was their backyard. There was nothing to be afraid of. Because of their experience, they thought they should continue on into the storm without waking Jesus from His sleep.

So many of us, because of our medical knowledge, scientific background, or experience, choose not to awaken Jesus during life's storms. We paddle on, losing the *very* thing God knows we could never save, and that's ourselves. Even Christians choose to live a life with a sleeping Jesus. They wear the cross of Jesus around their necks but do not invite Him into their storms. I hear Christians say all kinds of things like "I've got this! I've been through this before!" and "God will never give you more than you can handle." That last one irks me because it simply isn't true.

At a party once I was talking with a young woman who was going through a divorce. She had met the love of her life online and married her Prince Charming. She soon found out he was not. He was a liar and a cheater, and she thought she had been poisoned. As I listened, she bawled her eyes out. A well-meaning Christian woman standing nearby attempted to comfort her with these words, "God will never give you more than you can handle." That is the worst advice ever and a load of crap! Clearly, that woman had never read the story of Job. There are many things in this life you can't handle. Having the love of your life try to end your life is one of them. As a matter of fact, I find most days to be more than I can handle. The good news is we don't have to handle anything alone. We just have to wake the sleeping Jesus. But in your story, Jesus is not the one sleeping—you are.

Like so many, the brave fools on the Sea of Galilee paddled on, hoping the weather would change. Convincing themselves things would work out if they kept doing what they had always done. Talking to themselves, saying they had been through worse. I imagine James and John looking at Peter, asking, "We've been through worse, right? This is gonna work out, right?" There are some things positive thinking can't change, and the weather is certainly one of them! The wind howled, and the waves rose.

That's what life does. Storms don't send one wave and then apologize. They just keep coming.

The waves kept crashing, and the disciples kept rowing. They did all they could, and things got worse. Faithfully paddling out into the darkness. Have you ever been there? Done everything right, and things *still* went horribly wrong? Sometimes people eat right, never smoke, exercise daily, and still get lung cancer.

The first thing to go in a storm is the lights in the sky. No moon and no stars to light the way. Then the waves. Soaking your torches, knocking you around, and then filling the boat. Water was pouring in faster than our twelve friends could pour it out. They were drenched and trapped on a sinking ship.

Meanwhile, Jesus was sound asleep at the stern—the boat's back end, for my land-loving friends—dreaming of God knows what. Finally, when the disciples realized they were doomed, they shook Jesus and woke Him. The disciples screamed at Jesus, asking if He even cared that they would all die. Jesus said, "What?" Just kidding, He heard them the first time; He always does. If you are ready to cry out, Jesus is ready to listen! No matter where you are, Jesus *can* hear you from where He is. But like the disciples, we question whether Jesus even cares.

DOES GOD CARE?

It's bad enough to go through something like battling cancer, an unexpected death, or divorce and feel like you're losing your mind. It's even worse if you think no one cares. It's unbearable to feel like God doesn't care. So many of the psalms in the Bible are prayers where the author expressed feelings of abandonment by God. How quickly even the most faithful believers can feel this way! Life can go from a pleasure cruise to the *Titanic* in one phone call or conversation.

I never thought I would get so low as to question whether God cared, but in my midthirties, I did. I was overwhelmed by the storms of life, and I was sinking. When you are young, you have hopes and dreams of what life could be like. At some point, reality will punch you right in the face, and one day reality hit me—hard.

I planted a church when I was twenty-six. It was difficult, and I wasn't ready. About five years in, I hated being a pastor. I had hired friends and family to work for me, but it didn't work out. I lost friends and relationships and then started to lose my mind. My wife's father had recently died of cancer, just months after I led him to Christ. We had three young children. I was depressed, alone, and overwhelmed. I vividly remember being at the end of myself, sitting alone in my pickup truck, slamming my fist repeatedly into the passenger seat. I had answered God's call to start a church, but the waves were too big and too many.

I'd also been feeling horribly sick. At first, I was tired, and then, for months, I got worse. I had been to the doctor dozens of times, seen multiple specialists, and been tested for diseases I couldn't pronounce. I knew I was sick, but the doctors didn't have a name to label my condition.

Finally, I broke. Sitting in my truck, I screamed at God, "I am dying! Do You even care?"

Since then, I have heard others scream in this way. I call it the "soul cry." But the first time I heard the soul cry, it was coming out of my own mouth. Most of it was raw and real, but some of it was pretty offensive. I am not proud of everything I said or how I said it. God should be honored, and some of what I said was not honorable. But I was desperate. I told God I couldn't go on like this, and for the first time in my life, I thought about ending it all.

I didn't hear anything from God that day. The only noise was my pathetic, juvenile tantrum telling God I didn't like this life and that He was *terrible* at His job of being God. I couldn't feel Him at all. I could feel only my pain. I went home with no relief, no word, and no direction. I had screamed at God, and God had remained silent.

The storm was not over. More waves were coming.

When I arrived home, my wife, Tammy, was busy with our three young children. We greeted each other with a brief kiss and typical married pleasantries. She asked how my day was. I lied and said it was fine. After some more small talk, she said the doctor's office had left a message on the answering machine. My doctor, who I had seen many times, was a great doctor who truly wanted to help and was baffled about the root cause of my condition. He had ordered so many tests, I honestly had no idea on which test he was following up.

One of my many symptoms was severe throat pain. I would preach on Sunday, and my voice would be hoarse until Thursday. It was terribly painful week after week— shouting on Sunday and whispering until Thursday. I was a preacher, and it was my job to preach every week.

I called the doctor the next day, and our conversation was brief and to the point. He said the MRI showed something that looked like a tumor in my throat. It was rather large and low, so they would need to do immediate surgery to biopsy it. "I'm sorry, Matt," he continued. "But we may have found out what's wrong. We will need further tests to confirm, but based on the tumor's density and position, there is a chance it's cancer." He apologized again and said he hated to give me such alarming news, especially to someone so young. You *know* your life is bad when your situation makes a doctor feel bad for you.

I don't remember much after that. I went numb. I felt like cancer was everywhere, and I was overwhelmed. My wife's dad had just died of cancer. One of our pastors at Sandals Church was battling stage 4 kidney cancer. I shared the news with my wife and brother, and they rallied our church to start praying. They prayed, and I pouted.

My surgery was scheduled for ten days later. I was a wreck. I wasn't full of faith but instead full of fear. I had thought nothing could be worse than not knowing what was wrong with me, but this seemed worse. I went from a functioning depressed person to a nonfunctioning one. I was consumed with anger—aimed mainly at God. I thought God was not good, and this was not fair! He had called me to be a pastor. What is the point of being a preacher if you have no voice? I was in fight-or-flight mode, and I chose flight.

My wife's grandparents had a house in Palm Springs that was not being used. I told Tammy I needed time to think and pray. The truth was, I needed an escape. I'm not proud of what I did. With the word *cancer* hanging in the air, I left Tammy and our three young children and went to Palm Springs to be alone.

As I quickly packed my car and left, I told Tammy I was taking a vow of silence for a week. She didn't know what that was, and neither did I. I had never heard of anyone taking a vow of silence, and to be totally honest, I'm never silent! Not even when I'm alone. I talk all day long, preferably to others. If no one is available, I talk to myself. My children think it's weird; I just think it's me.

Since this was the early 2000s, we didn't have a way to text, so I told Tammy I would email her every day. I would love to say that God told me to take the silence vow, but He hadn't. In my mind, it was what I was supposed to do.

The first couple of days were peaceful. In the winter Palm Springs is like heaven. I walked and prayed and read Scripture all day. The world slowed, and on day three God spoke. Just kidding. I got bored on day three. There is only so much of Palm Springs I could take.

So on day three, I headed north to Joshua Tree National Park, ready to rattle and hum. I had a great day hiking—just me, my Bible, and the band U2. The change of scenery was just what I needed. Joshua Tree isn't that far from Palm Springs, but it feels like a different planet. I enjoyed my day and headed back to Palm Springs.

On my way out of the park, a police officer pulled me over. I used to get pulled over all the time. As a young pastor, I had long hair that I thought made me look like Jesus, but police and almost everyone else thought I looked like trouble. Don't judge the cops. Everywhere I went, people would offer me weed or ask me if I had any. Guess they didn't get the Jesus vibe I was going for. Whenever I returned to my small Christian college, someone always tried to share Christ with me. So cops thought I looked like a stoner, and Christians thought I looked like someone who needed to be saved.

When I pulled over, I tried to motion to the cop that I couldn't speak. He said, "No problem." About five minutes later, another police officer showed up who was a sign language interpreter. About two minutes into the unsuccessful hand conversation, I was about to be cuffed because they believed I was stoned and messing with them. So there I was, days from throat surgery. I hadn't spoken to my wife, and now I was headed to jail. I know what you are thinking: *Why not just talk?*

Because I take vows seriously, and I wanted God to know I was serious! I didn't go to jail. Another officer showed up and, by the grace of God alone, recognized me, and they let me go. They didn't understand why I wasn't speaking, but I was free and headed back to Palm Springs.

Remember what I said about waves? They kept coming.

I got an email that night from my wife saying she wasn't happy. She was scared about my surgery, angry about my distance, confused about my silence, and exhausted with our young children. She asked me to call her. But I couldn't. I had made a vow. A stupid vow at that point, but a vow nonetheless.

The next couple of days seemed like an eternity. I got angry. I stopped praying and reading my Bible. I just sat there waiting for the week to end. Tammy didn't email me the last two days, and I didn't blame her.

My week of silence was almost over. I had heard nothing from God, and then I heard nothing from Tammy. My surgery was in two days. I was ready to give up and give in.

Then I noticed an email in my inbox. It was from someone I knew of, but at the time I had no idea he knew of me. The email was from a pastor I admired. I never learned how he heard about my suffering or surgery, but I was grateful someone had told him. God hadn't spoken to me at all that week. God was as silent as I was—but His messenger was not. I needed a word, so God sent one. He sent a pastor.

That's what God does sometimes—sends His words through others. The pastor's words were not long, but they were powerful. The opening sentences of his email are forever etched in my memory:

Matt, praying for your surgery. God is with you; learn whatever you can during this time.

After I read those words, I cried. I prayed out loud. I immediately went home and spoke to my wife. The next day I went in for surgery.

That pastor's words spoke to me, as I am hoping this book will speak to you. That pastor was not Jesus, but he knew Jesus. I am not Jesus, but I have come to know Him. As his words did for me, I hope this book will awaken you to Jesus. There is more to Jesus than you know.

GOD WITH US

Matthew began his gospel about Jesus with another name for Jesus—Immanuel, meaning "God with us" (1:23). The disciples had to face the storm to truly discover who they had in the boat. This is the same lesson I had to learn. No matter how scary the storm you are going through, know that God is with you.

This is the first miracle you need to be aware of—the miracle of God's presence. He will never leave you; He is greater than the storm you currently face.

In the disciples' story, Jesus slept. In your story, Jesus is not sleeping, but maybe you have been. No matter who you are, where you have been, or what you are battling, you need to awaken to the reality of who Jesus really is. Because the truth is, God is with you in the boat, feeling the wind and the waves with you. He knows what you are going through, but He wants you to wake up and realize that He is with you. *God is with you!*

I pray this book helps you to learn whatever you can. I pray that you wake up.

PRAY

Lord Jesus, help me to wake up to the reality of who You are. There are times when I don't feel Your presence. Lord, I trust that You are there, but I need to feel You. I need to see Your power. Storms rage all around me. Please show me that You are stronger. Help me to learn whatever I can. I pray this in Your name, amen.

WATCH

REFLECT

1. Describe a storm that made you feel as if God didn't care about you.
2. What are the storms in your life that rattle you the most?
3. How has God used someone to let you know He cares about your situation?
4. Have you ever made a vow that made things worse? How did you fix it?
5. Jesus invited the disciples into the boat when He knew there was a storm coming. Why might Jesus be allowing you to go through your storm?

THREE

WAKING UP TO THE MIRACULOUS

AWAKE, O SLEEPER . . .

AND CHRIST WILL SHINE ON YOU.
EPHESIANS 5:14

Waking up from anesthesia after my throat surgery was bizarre. The first thing I remember is that I wasn't lying down. I was sitting straight up in my hospital bed. I wasn't drowsy at all. I was awake. *Wide awake.* I felt like I had just downed about six cups of coffee and topped that off with a Monster Energy drink. My heart was racing, and I was in a room full of bright lights.

At first, I thought it must be heaven, but then I noticed the room contained several people lying motionless on their beds. Was I dreaming? Or just dead? My eyes could not focus, but I saw a figure moving over one of the beds next to mine. That figure turned, looked at me, and screamed in my face, "You're not supposed to be awake!" Then the voice said sternly, "Lie down!"

The nurse helped me lie back down and went to get the doctor. Usually people take at least an hour to wake up after being under anesthesia. I had awoken in minutes and startled her, and she had scared me. A few moments later, the surgeon said the same thing as the nurse: "You should not be awake yet." But I was.

With a gravelly voice I asked him if the surgery had been a success. He smiled, and to my shock said, "No." I wondered why he said it with a big grin. He went on to explain that the surgery was not a success because he had found nothing.

"Nothing?" I whispered through my dry and cracked lips.

"Nothing," he said.

The surgeon went on to tell me that whatever was on the MRI was not there when he opened me up. He followed that up with, "Pastor Brown, MRIs are good, but my eyes are better." He said my throat was sore because he was "thorough." Looking around me at all the medical professionals who had gathered, I asked how this could be. The surgeon smiled and said, "You're the pastor; *you* tell me."

That day forever awakened me to the healing power of Jesus. While I was asleep, He was working. I had put *all* my faith in a surgeon who, in his words, had done nothing. But Jesus had done something. And it's something I believe He wants to do in and through you.

TIME TO WAKE UP

You may have been asleep, as I was, to the healing power of Jesus. But for healing to happen, you need to wake up. Like the storm faced by the twelve disciples in our previous chapter, the big waves in my life had overcome my small faith.

The real depth of our faith is revealed in the height of the wave we face. I thought I was done, just as the twelve disciples did in their sinking boat. All I could see was my end, but Jesus was just getting started. It wasn't my time to die or theirs. It was time to start living by faith. It was time to wake up.

When the disciples thought they were about to die, they said the most important words a person could ever speak: "Save us, Lord" (Matthew 8:25). The disciples were worried Jesus was asleep. They thought He was unaware of their situation and unconcerned about their fate. I want you to know that no matter what you go through, God sees and cares for you. Jesus is not asleep to your suffering. He is right there with you in your boat.

As Christians we often seem unaware of Jesus' power in our lives. So many of us are asleep to who Jesus really is. We are just Christians on cruise control. Our faith does not come from pretending the storm is not real or scary. Our faith comes from learning our God *is* real and present amid our storm.

I thought I was strong in my faith, but the storm revealed my weakness. I thought my time had come. But it was not my time to die; it was my time to believe. Not to believe in Jesus for who *I* thought He was but for who *He* knows Himself to be. I had to almost lose my life to truly deepen my faith.

For the first time, I experienced more of Jesus than I had known. I had known Him as Savior, but I had never known Him as Healer. I believed He had healed people in the Bible, but I didn't really believe He would heal me. But that is what He did. It's been more than twenty years since that surgery. I haven't had cancer or any problem with my voice since. I was completely healed, and I believe Jesus can do the same for you.

The disciples had to come close to losing their lives on the Sea of Galilee so they could find their faith. The disciples cried out, "Save us, Lord," and Jesus did. The verb translated as "save" in this verse is *soson* from the root word *sozo* in Greek. Greek is the original language of the New Testament. *Sozo* does not always mean "save." It can be and is translated in other verses as "heal." In the Bible, the words "save us" can be translated as "heal us."

Here are a few examples where the root word *sozo* is translated as "healed" in Scripture:

- In Matthew 9:22, Jesus described the healing miracle of a woman suffering physically for over twelve years. He said to the woman, "Daughter, your faith has *healed* you" (NIV).
- In Mark 10:52, Jesus said to a blind man, "Go . . . your faith has *healed* you" (NIV).
- In the Gospel of Luke, Luke the doctor used *sozo* to describe the miracle not just of saving a soul but of healing a person's body. In Luke 8:50, Jesus said to a

desperate father, "Don't be afraid; just believe, and she will be *healed*" (NIV).

I believe the Holy Spirit inspired the writers of these three gospels to use the word *sozo* for a reason. *Sozo* perfectly describes what God wants to do through your life and mine. As Christians, we can ask to be *saved*, and we can ask to be *healed*. The word *sozo* can mean either.

Jesus did not just come to save your soul but also to heal your heart, mind, and body so you could learn to love Him with all you truly are. Christians worldwide worship Jesus as our Savior but have forgotten that He is also our Healer. As Christians, we must have the faith to believe not only that He can save but also that He can heal. We must believe that He can save us from our sins and that He can save us from our storms.

> We must believe that He can save us from our sins and that He can save us from our storms.

WHY DON'T WE BELIEVE?

In the story we saw in the previous chapter, notice that before Jesus calmed the storm, He confronted the disciples' lack of faith. When the disciples woke Jesus, they begged Him, "Save us, Lord; we are perishing" (Matthew 8:25). In Mark's account of this event, the disciples said, "Don't you care that we're going to drown?" (4:38 NLT).

Jesus' response was amazing, and many people miss this key point: *before He spoke to the storm, Jesus spoke to the disciples*. What He yelled over the thrashing waves and the howling wind is something you need to hear amid your storm. It's something we all need to hear. Jesus responded to their question, "Why don't You care?" with His own question: "Why don't you believe?" Jesus said to the disciples, "Why are you afraid, O you of little faith?" (Matthew 8:26).

The problem, according to Jesus, was not the vast waves but their little faith. This is everyone's issue. It is not the name of your storm; it's that you have forgotten the name of the Person in your boat. Once you truly answer the question, "Who then is this, that even the wind and the sea obey him?" (Mark 4:41), you will find your faith and forever be done with your fear.

No matter what you are facing, no matter the prognosis, there is only one thing for you to learn in this storm. That one thing is to believe in Jesus for who He knows Himself to be. Jesus was experiencing the same waves, wind, and darkness on that boat, yet He slept like a baby. Why? Because He knew who He was and what He was capable of.

> **Jesus has not abandoned you in your storm but wants to reveal His power to you in the midst of it.**

Jesus is allowing your current storm to howl and rage not so you will *lose* your faith but so that you will *find* it. If you have faith, He's allowing the storm so you can deepen it. Jesus has not abandoned you in your storm but wants to reveal His power to you in the midst of it.

All true disciples must meet Him in this way. Jesus invited the twelve disciples to experience Him on a new level. Suffering is just another level.

The original twelve disciples were like so many Christians today. They were certain they knew Jesus. After all, they had heard Him preach. They had preached in His name. They had shared meals with Him. They had walked and talked with Him almost every day. They didn't just know the public Jesus; they knew the private Jesus. But even with this front-row, VIP access to Him, the disciples struggled to uncover the truth about Jesus. They were called as disciples upon the shores, but they became apostles in the storm. You see, believing in Jesus is easy when everything in life is great. Still believing in Jesus when everything falls apart is another thing entirely. The disciples *knew* Jesus of Nazareth, but they would *meet* Jesus from heaven on the Sea of Galilee.

If you are feeling overwhelmed by your current storm, know that Jesus did not come to take you down. He came to wake you up. He wants to wake you up to faith. Not only so that He can save you, but so that He can heal you and ultimately send you out as someone who knows Jesus. After all, He is Lord not just over the Sea of Galilee; He is Lord over all that is.

GOING FROM THE SEA
TO THE MOUNTAIN

For us to wake up, we will have to take a journey up. Our storms and suffering can take down our vision of Jesus. We don't just want to know Him in our storm; we want to see Him in His glory. For that to happen, we must go from a sea to a mountain because Jesus is the Lord of both.

In Mark 9, that's exactly what happened. Jesus took three of the twelve disciples to the top of a mountain and left the other nine below. We don't know why He left them. We can speculate it was their lack of faith, or perhaps they were not yet ready to know Jesus on another level.

Jesus took Peter, James, and John to the top of the mountain. These men were just as terrified on this mountain as they had been on the sinking ship. I love how Luke presented this event. He said, "Now Peter and those who were with him were heavy with sleep, but *when they became fully awake* they saw his glory" (v. 32).

That should be what we all want. But to achieve that, we can't sleepwalk through our Christian faith. We need to become fully awake. Some of us sleep through sermons and fall asleep when we pray, but I beg you not to fall asleep to this. This story is called the *transfiguration*, which is a big, fancy word that means a change of appearance. I wish it was not called this because Jesus did not change; He never does. It should be called the *revelation*. It was when Peter, James, and John got to see Jesus as He was.

The storm on the sea ended with a big question: "Who then is this, that even the wind and the sea obey?" The story of the transfiguration is a giant statement: "*This* is who the wind and the waves obey!" This is not where Jesus was changed but where He was revealed!

Mark's gospel begins this story with the fact that Jesus wanted to be alone with these three disciples (9:2).

They were handpicked to know Jesus on a deeper level. His clothes became radiant, brighter than anything the disciples had ever seen. Luke's gospel adds that the face of Jesus transformed (9:29), and Matthew's gospel adds that it became as bright as the sun (17:2)! The three disciples saw Jesus speaking with Moses and Elijah. They were overwhelmed and uncertain of what to do. Suddenly, a cloud appeared. Not a cloud like in the storm but a cloud of God. The cloud overshadowed them, and a voice that came out of the cloud said, "This is my beloved Son; listen to him" (Mark 9:7).

There is no longer a question about who Jesus is. Even the wind and the sea obey Him because He is the very Son of God. God said from within the cloud that He is to be listened to. That's what the wind and the sea did, and that's what I want *us* to do. We all need to listen to Jesus. Because whether we are on the mountain or in the boat, the voice that often seems to scream the loudest is not the God *above* us but the voice of fear *within* us.

Jesus asked Peter, James, and John to keep His transfiguration to themselves until after He rose from the dead. They were asked to keep quiet. But you and I have been commanded to shout who Jesus is from the rooftops!

OUR STRUGGLE TO BELIEVE

Peter, James, and John left this amazing mountaintop experience and immediately had to face the realities of life on earth. Real life is tough. When they got to the bottom of the mountain, they found the other nine disciples engaged in a heated argument with a man with a sick son who had come to see Jesus. I think so many of our arguments about healing and miracles would end if, instead of trying to make a point, we just pointed people to Jesus.

Jesus showed up, and everyone shut up. Jesus asked them what they were arguing about. No one said anything. His disciples and His critics were silent. Finally, the hurting father spoke up and said, "Teacher, I brought my son to you, for he has a spirit that makes him mute. And whenever it seizes him, it throws him down, and he foams and grinds his teeth and becomes rigid. So I asked your disciples to cast it out, and they were not able" (Mark 9:17–18).

This is every believer's worst fear: we will step out in faith, and our prayers won't make a difference.

We don't know exactly what the argument had been about before Jesus showed up. Probably about whether disciples could even do miracles; after all, it hadn't worked. At some time in your life, you will pray, and from your perspective, it won't work. But I want you to know that prayer always works. It may not have the desired outcome you prayed for, but your prayer worked. When you pray, every time you pray, you are heard. This is the purpose of prayer: to have your voice *heard* by God, not to get your way with God.

These nine disciples tried to cast out the demon tormenting the boy, but it did not help. You have to feel for them. They were not picked to go to the mountain, and now they were being mocked in the valley! But Jesus did not just challenge His disciples; He challenged all who were present.

Because the nine disciples' problem is our problem. They all lacked faith. Jesus turned to the crowd and said to everyone standing there, "O faithless generation, how long am I to be with you? How long am I to bear with you? Bring him to me" (v. 19).

Sometimes the problem with our faith is not that we don't believe in miracles; it's that we struggle to believe in Jesus. These disciples saw Jesus do amazing thing after amazing thing, and they still didn't get it. Unfortunately, that's how many believers live out their entire Christian lives—without real faith in Christ.

Jesus turned His attention away from the crowd and focused on the hurting father. You have to feel for this guy. His son had many challenges in a world with little health care or medical understanding. It is one thing to see people suffer; it's another thing to see your child suffer. I believe losing a child is the worst thing a person can go through. That's why God went through it—not just to save you but to truly "get" you. To understand and experience human pain and suffering.

Jesus asked the father, "How long has this been happening to him?" The father answered, "From childhood" (Mark 9:21). The broken, beaten father said, "But if you can do anything, have compassion on us and help us" (v. 22). Jesus suddenly shifted from compassion to frustration and replied, "'If you can'!" (v. 23). Remember how our story on the mountain began? God said, "This is my beloved Son; *listen to him*" (v. 7).

This is where I challenge you not to pay attention to what I am writing, what you have heard, or what you believe or have been taught about Jesus when it comes to healing. I want you to look carefully at the words of Jesus. His answer to this father will change the way you pray, and it will change the way you live.

Jesus said, "Everything is possible for one who believes" (v. 23 NIV). The key word to what Jesus was saying here is "possible." Jesus did not say that everything is *promised* for one who believes. He said everything is *possible*. Prayer does not command God; it makes a request of God. When we pray, we are called to believe, without doubt, not in what God *will* do but in what God *can* do.

Jesus was not upset because the father didn't know what would happen. He was upset because the father was unsure if Jesus *could* make anything happen. Anyone who tells you they know what God is going to do when it comes to healing is usually wrong. They don't know because they are not God.

Prayer is a request for a miracle, not an order for one. We don't give God orders; we take them. Our job is not to believe for a miracle but to believe in the One who is miraculous! Luckily for this father, the Miracle Worker was standing right before him. The father said what we all need to say to see more of heaven's miraculous power on earth. He said, "I believe." But he said it a little too quickly and immediately made a correction because he realized he *didn't* really believe it. He added, "Help my unbelief!" (v. 24). He recognized there was a gap between what he had *proclaimed* and what he actually *thought*.

This same gap exists in believers who shout in an emotional frenzy, "I believe!" We all want to believe, but we all need help with our unbelief. At some point, we will have an experience like this man had. You trust God but don't get what you believe you need, and it will challenge your faith in God.

The story of this suffering man with a deeply troubled son began with these words: "Teacher, I brought my son so you could heal

> **Prayer is a request for a miracle, not an order for one.**

him" (v. 17 NLT). This is important because Jesus had just arrived back from being on the mountain with God. So when this man brought his son to Jesus, all he got were the imperfect disciples, who seemed only to make things worse.

I encourage you not to doubt God because you believed in someone who claimed to represent Him. It's easy to get disappointed when we trust the wrong people. Don't believe in the one wearing a religious uniform; believe in the One who transformed in front of Peter, James, and John. People are broken, but Jesus was broken for you.

That's why the man was struggling. He had the faith to travel and seek healing for his son. That's something. But his faith led only to disappointment and arguments. Sometimes that's what happens when we seek a miracle from Jesus. We just get broken people who create a bigger mess. It's easy to be discouraged, and I don't blame people who are. The good news is, you don't have to go through people who claim to know Jesus; you can go directly to Him. Again, not believing in what He *will* do but believing in what He *can* do. When we do that, Jesus said everything is possible.

The boy's father said what he thought he was supposed to say to Jesus, and then he said what he *needed* to say to

> **We need the faith to ask for our miracle and the faith to believe in the One who can do the miracle.**

Him. That's what you and I need to do in every situation for which we need a miracle. We need the faith to ask for our miracle and the faith to believe in the One who can do the miracle. I don't know how God will respond to the first part of your request, but I do know how He will respond to the second part. He will help you with your faith in Him every time you ask. This is a miracle that can happen every day!

The boy's father asked to be helped with his unbelief, and Jesus did. Because the commotion had drawn an even larger crowd, one that was growing every second, Jesus turned to the boy. Jesus did not want this event to be a public spectacle but a personal miracle for a father and a son. So He acted quickly.

Turning to the boy, Jesus commanded that he be healed. The boy had seizures, was deaf, and could not speak. He had suffered his entire life. The boy's issue was not just physical but spiritual. Jesus commanded the evil spirit to come out. The spirit obeyed Jesus but shook the boy violently as it left. The boy shook with such violence that the Bible says he became "like a corpse" (v. 26).

Many people thought that Jesus had not helped him but killed him. Jesus calmly reached down, grabbed the boy's hand, and lifted him up. The boy stood on his own, seeing the crowd as he looked upon the people and heard the sound of praise. There were two miracles that day: the miraculous healing of a young man and the miracle of faith—not just the faith to believe that Jesus could save but that Jesus could heal.

The miracle was over, but the lesson was not. Jesus and the disciples needed a break from the crowds. It had been a long walk for Jesus, Peter, James, and John, but it had been an even longer day for the nine disciples. They had been publicly embarrassed and verbally attacked.

As they entered the house, they asked Jesus a great question we should all ask. They wanted to know why they couldn't heal the boy and drive out the demon. Jesus did not minimize or put down their question. He answered it. He said, "This kind cannot be driven out by anything but prayer" (v. 29).

In the next chapter, we will learn to pray for the miraculous.

PRAY

Jesus, please help me believe not only that You can save but also that You can heal. Help me to trust You. Remind me that my role isn't to believe in what You will do but in what You can do. I pray this in Your name, amen.

WATCH

REFLECT

1. Describe a time when you were surprised by a miracle.
2. As believers, we all have faith *and* struggle with our faith at the same time. Like the father who needed faith for a miracle for his son, where do you need to ask Jesus to help you believe?
3. Jesus took only three of the twelve disciples to the Mount of Transfiguration. What in your life might be keeping you below with the nine?
4. When Jesus healed the boy, things got scary. How have you allowed fear to keep you from praying for the miraculous?
5. On the mountain, God said, "This is my beloved Son; listen to him" (Mark 9:7). What might Jesus be speaking to you right now?

FOUR

LEARNING TO PRAY FOR MIRACLES

"LORD, TEACH US TO PRAY."
LUKE 11:1

We need miracles every day—often when we least expect it. Because every day feels like any other day until it isn't.

It was a typical sweltering summer day in Southern California. Tammy and I were having a pool party in our new home to celebrate my sister-in-law's birthday and the recent birth of my niece Junell, who was just a few months old. She was perfect—a full head of the most beautiful ice-blonde hair and big, bright-blue eyes. She reminded me so much of how my brother looked when he was young. The day was incredible. We had the warm sun and a cool swimming pool. Tammy and I were enjoying our new home full of the people we loved and looking forward to many more parties just like this one.

Then out of nowhere, a bloodcurdling scream instantly changed everything. It was my sister-in-law. She screamed, "The baby! The baby is not breathing!" I froze with fear as I looked at my little niece. Her body was blue. My sister-in-law's beautiful, long brown hair was tightly clenched in Junell's tiny fist, as if she were fighting to hold on to life.

My brother scrambled and pried his daughter's little fingers one by one from his wife's hair, placed Junell on the ground, and began CPR. Her body was lifeless and not responding to CPR. What we didn't know was that we were making things worse. When you do CPR on a baby that young, you have to be careful. Adult lungs are strong, but little new lungs are not. In trying to blow air into her little lungs, we ended up blowing little holes in them.

My brother screamed, "This isn't working; we've got to go!" The hospital was just down the street. It was almost a straight shot, so instead of waiting for an ambulance to arrive, I said, "Just go," and assured him I'd bring my sister-in-law.

My brother sped off, and I turned and heard my sister-in-law mumble, "My baby," as she collapsed helplessly on my front lawn.

The party was over, and real life had smacked us in the face. I scooped up my sister-in-law and drove her to the hospital. Our house was filled with friends from our church, so car after car followed closely behind me. When we arrived at the hospital, there was a frantic rush of nurses and doctors scrambling to save the precious baby's life. We were immediately met by a nurse who ushered us into a meditation room. (Side note: Most hospitals in California no longer call them "prayer rooms," just "meditation rooms"—maybe that is why we see so few miracles there.)

As we waited helplessly, church members started piling in. Soon it was standing room only, and people spilled out the door into the hall. We were all in disbelief that we could lose Junell. Some time passed, and my brother walked in slowly, oblivious to anyone else in the room. He was in shock and looked as pale as a ghost. I was sure he was going to say Junell was dead.

My brother looked at his wife and said, "She's still not breathing." Then he leaned in close to her and whispered, "It doesn't look good."

I don't know how long we sat there, but that's exactly what we did. A bunch of believers, sitting in disbelief. Each minute brought a new person into the room and more doubt that Junell would live.

Then someone stood up and asked, "Shouldn't we be praying?" Almost half of our tiny congregation was at the hospital by then. Right there in the meditation room and overflowing into the hallway, we all got on our knees and prayed, begging God for a miracle. This type of tragedy was a new thing for our young church. Most of our members were in their late teens or early twenties. I was probably the oldest person in the room who prayed that day, but we all prayed despite our age and lack of wisdom. We cried out to God. Every person prayed from their heart as we went around the room, and I closed with these words:

"Heal her, Jesus. Please bring her back. In Jesus' name we pray, amen."

The second—I mean the *exact second*—I said amen, a doctor, one of the many working on her, burst through the door and said, "We got her back!" He told us she was not entirely out of the woods yet, but she had a pulse, was breathing, and things looked promising for a full recovery. Then he said, "Keep praying!" The room went wild with praise.

My brother and his wife were in the center of the cheering crowd. I read his lips as he looked at the ceiling and quietly said, "Thank You, Jesus," over and over again.

Two things happened that day. First, we experienced an absolute horror. It took months to get over the trauma of what we saw. The second was that we witnessed an absolute, verifiable miracle. The doctor said so. Junell was gone, but God brought her back through the hands of diligent doctors and His people's prayers. I wrote a thank-you letter to Jesus and my niece Junell in my journal that day. I wrote, "Thank you for teaching me that prayer works, and miracles can happen."

As I have reflected on that day many times over the years, I have wondered why it took us so long to think about prayer. I know we were in shock. But our shock hadn't kept us from talking; it just seemed to keep us from praying. I have seen this play out countless other times when Christians are in crisis. Instead of turning to God in prayer, we turn to news reporters or each other. I'm not sure why we do this, but sharing is not praying. It's in times like this—when we really need a miracle—that we need to turn to God in prayer.

LEARNING TO PRAY LIKE JESUS

The first reason we struggle with prayer is that prayer can be intimidating. This was true even for the disciples. As we saw in the previous chapter, they did not know how to pray in a way that would help the boy afflicted with a spiritual and physical illness. Just like the disciples, if we want to learn how to help people who need miracles, we must learn to pray like Jesus.

Jesus taught the disciples how to pray, as recorded in two of the Gospels. The shorter version is in Luke (11:2–4), and the slightly longer version is in Matthew (6:9–13). I personally like Luke's version because it's brief, and it came in response to the disciples' request that Jesus teach them how to pray.

I can only imagine what it must have been like to hear Jesus pray. I have been fortunate enough to be around some of the great saints of the church. There is something special about people who know they are talking directly with God. I have felt intimidated to pray in front of these people. The good news is God has not called me or you to pray like anyone but Jesus. The disciples heard Jesus pray, and when He finished they were not insecure about how they prayed but desperate to learn to pray like Him.

One of the disciples spoke up and said, "Lord, teach us to pray" (Luke 11:1).

This one disciple knew what every disciple knew: we need to deepen our understanding of prayer. I'm sure the disciples had prayed many times before, but when they heard Jesus pray, they realized their prayers were missing something. Perhaps it was the same something that was missing when they tried to help the young boy. What I want you to notice is that Jesus did not correct them; He showed them how they should pray. Jesus wanted all His disciples to learn how to pray, so He said:

> "When you pray, say:
> 'Father,
> hallowed be your name,
> your kingdom come.
> Give us each day our daily bread.
> Forgive us our sins,
> for we also forgive everyone who sins
>   against us.
> And lead us not into temptation.'"
>   (vv. 2–4 NIV)

Now, I realize the translation I quoted above may be slightly different from the one you are used to, but it's probably close to what you know. I don't want you to get caught up in the slight differences but rather to focus on its brevity.

Pray Simply

The Lord's Prayer is not His prayer at all. It is to be our prayer, and the first thing I want you to notice is that it is incredibly short! It takes me between thirteen and fifteen seconds to pray it. I know because I have timed myself.

Many Christians are intimidated to pray because we feel like we have to go on and on. Many of us were taught the longer we pray, the better we are praying. Jesus actually taught exactly the opposite. He said, "And when you pray, do not keep on babbling like pagans, for they think they will be heard because of their many words" (Matthew 6:7 NIV). We don't have to pray forever. We just have to pray briefly for what we need.

Jesus affirmed what Solomon taught: when we speak to God, we should "let [our] words be few" (Ecclesiastes 5:2). Jesus said, "Your Father knows what you need before you ask him" (Matthew 6:8). God is not looking for information when we pray. He is looking for authentic faith.

Pray Authentically

The reason I did not choose a translation like the King James Version for the Lord's Prayer is that it's almost too beautiful. Authentic prayer is beautiful to God's ears but not to our own. Real prayer is rough! Sometimes a prayer that sounds like nonsense to us is a perfect prayer to God.

So many people, when they pray, try to sound like they are in a Shakespeare play. You don't need to change your voice when you pray. You don't have to use the words *thou*, *thy*, or *shall*; just use your ordinary language. If my kids came to me when they needed something and said, "Dearest Father, provider of our sustenance and valiant protector of thine home, we beseech thee to incline thy ear . . . ," I would start laughing. Prayer is not a joke, so just use the voice God gave you so that all of heaven knows who is talking. Jesus said that fake people who pray love to be heard by others and seen by people. When you pray, you want to be heard by *God*, so Jesus said to keep it real and use your real voice.

Pray Daily

Next, I want to point out the phrase "give us *each day*" (Luke 11:3 NIV). Jesus meant that we should come to God with our needs every day.

The best way to learn to pray is to practice praying. Anyone new to prayer will feel awkward at first. But know that all things feel awkward when we are just beginning. When you took your first steps, you were awkward. But you took them! You lost your balance and lost your step. You fell over and over. But today, if you can walk, you are probably an expert at walking. You do it every day without thinking about how you do it. So practice every day, and just as your parents on earth may have cheered you on as you learned to walk, your Father in heaven is cheering you on as you learn to pray! Practice praying privately first, and then build up your confidence to pray in public.

When Jesus taught His first disciples how to pray, He emphasized that private prayer must come first. He taught His disciples to pray in the privacy of their own rooms (Matthew 6:6). His advice to go into their rooms to pray does not mean we should never pray out loud in public. Jesus prayed out loud and in public all the time. But it is not the only time one should pray—to be seen as spiritual or holier-than-thou.

It would have been foolish for me to send everyone out

of the meditation room at the hospital and say, "Now, go home and pray." We didn't need a miracle at home in their rooms. We needed one right there in the hospital, so that's where we prayed! Not to be heard by those passing by but to be heard by our Father in heaven.

Pray Specifically

There are many things to learn from the Lord's Prayer, and many books have focused exclusively on it. I want to keep this chapter focused on praying for a miracle. So if it is a miracle that you are praying for, I encourage you to be as specific as possible.

What I believe Jesus meant when He said, "Give us this day *our daily bread*" (Matthew 6:11), is to ask for what you need to survive. That's your bread, so you should pray specifically for it! Tell your Father who is in heaven the specific bread you need. Tell Him what type of bread! Tell Him how many slices you need! If it's rent, say the specific amount you are looking for. I cannot tell you how many times I have prayed explicitly and seen God provide precisely what I needed. If you want a vague answer, pray a vague prayer.

I have prayed for small things, like when I was a pastor struggling financially. My wife and I had just bought a repossessed home. The home was a mess, and we could afford only so many improvements. We made a list of what we could and could not afford to fix. The list was *specific*. We decided we could not afford a stove. So I asked God for a stove. The next weekend I was a guest preacher at a church in Los Angeles. At the end of the church service, a man came up and said, "Pastor, this may sound strange, but I feel like God told me to buy you a stove." We went to Costco that day, and he bought us a brand-new one.

Specific prayer does not have to be small. I told my church leadership team that I wanted to open a new campus for our church in Orange County, California. I said I wanted it to be free. They all chuckled, but that's what we prayed for. Two months later, we received a property in Orange County for free. Your heavenly Father wants you to come to Him when you need a miracle. I do not promise millions of dollars, but I promise that you can pray and ask God, who has far more than millions, for whatever you need!

Confess Your Sins

The next thing I want you to see in the Lord's Prayer is the part about asking for forgiveness of sin and forgiving those who sin against us. There is nothing that blocks prayer like unconfessed sin.

My baby niece was brought back to life because God answered our prayer. Doctors were never sure what had happened to her. It was likely a heart attack caused by some sort of stroke. The event was traumatic for a tiny girl just a few months old. But that didn't end up being the greatest threat to her life. Her biggest challenge was the accidental damage to her lungs when we performed CPR.

She was too sick to remain in the hospital near our home. She needed to be transported to a better hospital with the ability to help babies. After being transported, she spent the next couple of weeks battling for her little life. But she was not fighting alone. She had an army of prayer warriors lifting up her small body every day before the Lord.

However, things did not improve; they got worse. That sometimes happens when we pray. If things don't immediately improve, stay encouraged and maintain faith. Remember, when Jesus told the father to bring Him the sick boy, things got worse before Jesus ultimately brought a miracle.

My baby niece got bad, really bad. So bad that my brother asked the hospital to allow pastors to come in and anoint her with oil, as the Bible instructs in James 5:14. I was so impressed with my brother's faith, and with the hospital for giving us permission to follow our faith. So we rallied pastors not just from our church but also from surrounding churches. We met at the hospital, put on sterile gowns, and washed our hands.

But before we went in to pray, my brother stopped us and said we first needed to confess any sin to God before we asked Him for a miracle. He read aloud, "Confess your sins to each other and pray for each other so that you may be healed" (James 5:16 NIV).

We wanted a miracle, so one by one, we began to confess our sins. I can't remember any of the sins confessed that day, but everyone had something they needed to get off their chest. The general theme of confession was to help us believe in what only God could do. These were pastors who, like the father in Mark 9, confessed we needed help believing that our prayers could do anything when the situation was so dire.

James did not promise a miracle but promised miraculous power when believers are freed from sin through confession. When we are free from sin on earth, we can be full of heaven's power, even if just for that moment. That's why James said, "The prayer of a righteous person is powerful and effective" (5:16 NIV).

> If you want power in your prayer, put confession of sin into practice in your life.

We *needed* God's power at that moment and wanted our prayer to be effective, so we confessed before we prayed. If you want power in your prayer, put confession of sin into practice in your life.

As we approached my niece, she was unconscious in a little oxygen tent. The tent helped to slowly press air into her fragile lungs. The hospital permitted us to remove the tent only long enough to pray. With doctors and nurses surrounding us as we prayed over her, we asked for complete healing in Jesus' name.

We prayed and anointed her with oil, and then something miraculous happened. She quickly grew stronger, and she began to breathe deeper. In a matter of hours, she was breathing on her own, free from all her tubes and in her mother's arms. It was a miracle—a total miracle.

My niece Junell has now graduated from college and has her whole life ahead of her. She is living proof of prayer's miraculous power. To this day, I run into doctors or nurses who heard about or saw the power of prayer that day in a NICU.

That's the power of prayer when we confess our sins. It's

why Jesus included instruction to confess our sins immediately after we pray for our daily bread. Prayer is about the miracle you need; confession is the miracle God desires. To unlock God's power in your prayers, you need both!

> **Prayer is about the miracle you need; confession is the miracle God desires.**

Approach God with Boldness

So many amazing things happened on the day we received that incredible miracle. One of them was my brother's boldness. He was going to do what he felt God was asking him to do no matter what! You and I should be bold like my brother.

In our previous chapter, we saw that the troubled boy's father was bold enough to seek a miracle from Jesus. He was bold enough to speak up even when Jesus' own disciples were silent. He was also bold enough to confess his unbelief. Jesus wants us to be bold. That's why He began the Lord's Prayer with the words "Our Father" and not "Our stranger" (Matthew 6:9). He is God Almighty in heaven, but He is also your dad on earth. He wants to hear your requests. He loves you, cares deeply for you, and wants you to call on Him boldly!

I don't know what kind of phone you have. I assume it's a smartphone. I love smartphones because when I was kid, you never knew who was calling until you picked up the phone and said hello. Now I know who is calling before I answer, and I only answer if I want to. Sometimes when work is heavy or life is crazy, I put my phone on Do Not

Disturb. This allows me to get away from my phone and get to the work I need to get done. This mode blocks everyone except for a few numbers I put in my Favorites.

Three of the numbers that are never blocked are my children's numbers. No matter where I am, they can reach me from where they are. Do you know why that is? Because I am their dad. They will have many people in their lives on earth but only one father. That's me, and I want them to call, especially if they need something important. But even more than that, I don't just want to take their call; I pay for their phone service. All of my kids are young adults, and it's difficult for them to make the money needed to pay all their bills. I pay their phone bill so they have no excuse if they ever need Dad.

Your heavenly Father has paid your phone bill so you can call on Him for free. This is why many translations of the Lord's Prayer say "debt" instead of "sin." Your sin debt has been paid by Jesus on His cross so that no matter where you are, day or night, you can call and He will answer. God will answer every time you pray.

Since we have this unique relationship with God, we need to approach Him with boldness. Because of Jesus, you and I have direct access to heaven. We have a Savior who understands what it's like to hurt because He understands what it's like to be human. In the book of Hebrews, the author explained the depth of this reality, this VIP access we have to God through Jesus. He said, "Let us come boldly to the throne of our gracious God. There we will receive his mercy, and we will find grace to help us when we need it most" (4:16 NLT).

You and I are commanded to come to God with boldness, especially when we need it the most! No matter what we need or how crazy our request is, as sons and daughters of the King, we will be heard and receive an answer. God answers every prayer that is ever prayed in one of three ways—yes, no, or wait. So you never have to wonder *if* God will answer. He will, every time. No matter what's happening in heaven, God stops to hear from you.

> God answers every prayer that is ever prayed in one of three ways— yes, no, or wait.

We may not know *how* God will answer our prayers, but we must never forget that He *always* will.

PRAY

Lord Jesus, teach me to pray. Help me to start where I am, and please teach me to pray as You did. Help me have the faith to believe that not only can You do all things but You hear and answer all my prayers. I pray this in Jesus' name, amen.

WATCH

REFLECT

1. Why do you think the Lord's Prayer is so short?
2. How can memorizing the Lord's Prayer help as you learn to pray on your own?
3. When would be the best time each day for you to schedule prayer?
4. Have you ever had an awful experience praying out loud? How can you move past that? Is there a way other believers might help you pray more confidently?
5. How does it make you feel to know God will hear and answer every prayer you pray?
6. The Lord's Prayer ends with "Don't let us yield to temptation" (Luke 11:4 NLT). What temptations do you face when it comes to prayer?

FIVE

ASKING GOD FOR A MIRACLE (BECAUSE HE CAN SAY YES)

"ASK, AND IT WILL BE GIVEN TO YOU."
MATTHEW 7:7

Life is not fair, but God is good. We never know what life will bring, but I have learned time and time again that I can bring whatever life throws at me directly to God.

In Matthew's teaching on the Lord's Prayer, he gave us a longer version and more instruction regarding prayer. Here, Jesus taught that we don't have to go on and on when we pray because our Father already knows what we need before we even ask. You might be wondering, *Then why even ask?* The answer, Jesus said, is that while God already knows what we need, we won't know what He will do about it until we ask. God is not in the business of answering prayers we do not pray. So no matter what you need, ask God for it.

He might say yes.

As a pastor, I have repeatedly seen God do miraculous wonders when I had lost all hope. Over the years, I have pastored thousands of people who have come through the doors of Sandals Church. Every one of them is special to God, but a certain few are dear to me. They are the ones who, through thick and thin, for better or worse, stayed with me when others didn't.

The challenge of starting a church when you are so young is that you have absolutely no idea what you are doing. My talent for speaking outweighed the depth of my faith. My vision for what God wanted to do *through* me was completely blind to what He first needed to do *in* me. So I am eternally grateful to God for His patience and for many people who followed me even when I was not yet the leader they needed me to be.

One of those people is Natasha. When Sandals Church first started, young people poured through our doors. As we grew, there were always more people than we had room for. Sandals Church moved locations thirteen times in the first three years. Our unofficial motto was, "Come worship with us if you can find us." Well, Natasha found us, and she stuck with us.

A brilliant young woman and a swimming star with a bright future, Natasha met the love of her life in high school and had dreams of marriage and children. One day, out of nowhere, she began feeling tired and unable to complete tasks that a few weeks prior had been easy for her. Even though she was in incredible shape, she was always fatigued. Something was wrong, terribly wrong.

At nineteen years old, she found out she had cancer.

Natasha was assured that her cancer was treatable. Being young and naive like most teenagers, she didn't worry too much about it. Her confident doctor assured her she would be done with cancer after one round—maybe two—of chemotherapy. She would then be free to go on with her life.

This was not the case.

Ten years later, Natasha sat in my office with tears in her eyes and asked a very valid question: "Why won't God heal me?" She'd fought cancer for ten years. She'd received the best treatments possible—some proven, some experimental. She had a doctor who cared for her and an attentive hospital staff. But now her doctor said there was no longer hope. Natasha was told she was just unlucky—they had no idea why her particular cancer was so stubborn to treatments that had worked for many others. There were no more treatments to try.

Natasha didn't understand. She was no longer a teenager and no longer naive. She knew very well that her life was on the line. After ten years of battling fiercely for her life, she had lost hope and the energy to keep fighting. She was at the end of her rope.

I had to concede that I didn't understand either. Natasha sat in my office, ravaged by years of chemotherapy, not looking like a young woman should. She was devastated by the ups and downs, all the promises that the next treatment (or the next) would be the one to cure her. Weeping, she handed me a picture—an MRI of her entire body. The image looked like a Dalmatian dog because her body was covered in black spots. I asked if the black spots were cancer, and she nodded. They were everywhere—clustered around many of the organs in her chest and abdomen.

She said, "I don't have long, Pastor. I need a miracle."

Natasha, myself, a few other pastors, and her husband bowed our heads in prayer, asking our Father in heaven for a miracle. We all prayed. It is only with her permission that I share what was said, which was so painful, raw, and heart-wrenching that it will stay with me forever. Natasha found her soul cry.

In chapter 2, I mentioned my own soul cry. A soul cry is when there is nothing left between you and God. You are done with the games; you have nothing to hide. You just need to be heard.

There is something powerful and haunting about a soul cry. Its sound makes every other noise in life disappear. As you realize the depth of suffering another person feels, your own problems and suffering seem shallow and insignificant. In these moments, you accept how incredibly blessed you are to have the life you have.

When I heard Natasha cry out to God, she no longer seemed frail. The room had to make space for her spirit as she spoke to our Father, who is Spirit. She yelled, "I don't want to die!" The first scream was powerful but simply made room for what was to follow. A lioness came out of her petite frame, and its voice rattled the room. "I don't want to die!" She began to beat the drum of her request before the King of kings and Lord of lords. Every downstroke in the drum of her voice led to another more thunderous beat. Natasha was going to be heard.

Even as the lone woman in the room, she grew fiercer with every request. "I am not ready to die!" she yelled.

To the observer, it may have looked like a wild woman screaming into the air. But as believers, we knew she was being heard by God. She became the pastor, and I became the student. We were all in awe of her strength and were moved to tears. We had no words. Nothing more needed to be added.

I anointed Natasha's forehead with oil and said, "Lord Jesus, I know You can hear her; I beg You to heal her; I pray this in Your holy name, amen."

Amen is a word we all say but few of us understand. It is a word so powerful it has never been changed. When the Bible was translated from Hebrew and Greek to Latin and English, most of the words it contains were translated. *Amen* was not. Amen is *amen* in Hebrew. It is *amen* in Greek. It is also *amen* in Latin and obviously in English as well. *Amen* means to agree that truth has been spoken. It means what we have said is real and raw. Some people play games when they speak to one another, but we should never play games when we talk with God.

Natasha had been real. She'd been raw. We all agreed with the prayer and believed that truth had been spoken, so I said amen.

It has now been years since that night we prayed, back

when Natasha was given only weeks to live. She is still alive and on staff at Sandals Church. She is here because when the hospital said there was no hope left, she went to the One who is the source of our hope!

Why do we pray? We pray because God might say yes. What do we have to lose when there is no other source of hope? Take a chance and reach for Jesus. There is real power in His name. He is God's one and only Son, and He *can* say yes.

I know it's hard to trust Jesus with your request. I realize that, like Natasha, you may have prayed for healing many times, and many times it might not have been granted. Don't give up! Jesus taught us to keep asking and to keep knocking on heaven's door for what we need. He said, "Keep on asking, and you will receive what you ask for. Keep on seeking, and you will find. Keep on knocking, and the door will be opened to you. For everyone who asks, receives. Everyone who seeks, finds. And to everyone who knocks, the door will be opened" (Matthew 7:7–8 NLT).

If you feel discouraged, remind yourself that your repeated prayers are prayers of obedience. There will be times when you feel unheard; you have to find the strength to pray through it. Again, I cannot promise you will get a yes, which agrees with what Jesus taught in this passage.

What are we seeking? An answer! What door do we want opened? Heaven's, so we can be heard! According to Jesus, if you keep asking, you will be answered. He is not guaranteeing the miracle you want, but you *will* receive the miracle you need.

That miracle is the miracle of being heard.

PRAY REPEATEDLY

Jesus was trying to teach us that righteousness comes from repetition. I heard this in Natasha's prayer. She wasn't praying some memorized, written, religious prayer. Instead she found the strength of her soul through the repetition of her words. God wants to hear your voice; this is not in question. The question is, Do we want to be heard? Jesus said that when we really want something, we should keep on asking. I want you to experience this: there's a unique power that often comes when we repeatedly call on the name of the Lord!

When my wife and I were in college, we had a tough breakup. We'd dated for almost two years, but our relationship was messy. I wasn't right with God, and I wasn't right with her, so I called it off. I broke up with Tammy, and I broke her heart. There hadn't been a single day in the previous two years when we hadn't spoken at least once. But now we didn't talk for an entire summer. As the summer ended, God began to open my eyes. The problem hadn't been us; it had been me.

I remember pulling her picture out of my drawer at work and placing it on my desk. Staring at it, I knew I had made a colossal mistake. I immediately called her. She answered and then hung up when she realized it was me. I called back, and she hung up again. So I called a third time, and the answer was the same: *click!* Finally, on the tenth call, she answered and said, "What do you want?"

On the first call, I would've had no idea how to answer that. But by the tenth time, I was ready. I said, "I was wrong to break up with you. I'm sorry; please forgive me." There was only silence on the other end, but she didn't hang up. I know now she was crying. We have now been married for twenty-seven years, and we have three amazing children. I am so glad I didn't give up. As I called over and over, I was not discouraged; I was awakened to something I really wanted and felt I needed. It took nine rejections to prepare me for her acceptance.

As you repeatedly seek the answer to your prayer, you will not grow weaker but stronger in your faith. Natasha was given only weeks to live, but as she repeated her request, she found new faith with each successive knock. She wasn't babbling; she was praying. Her words did not change, but the seriousness of them did. And God opened the door to more years of life. This is why Jesus said to keep knocking. So knock *repeatedly*.

When we have to pray repeatedly for a miracle, it's easy to get discouraged. I have often prayed with a wife or husband who has become tired of praying for their marriage. I have often heard the words, "Pastor, I don't think I can do it anymore." I will tell you the same thing I've told them: rely on God's strength and invite Him to do it through you. That's the amazing thing about prayer—when we don't have the strength to keep praying anymore, we can borrow God's! If you are tired, admit it; tell God. Say, "I'm tired. I can't keep asking anymore. My fists are blistered from knocking at Your door, Lord!"

When we have to come repeatedly before the Lord, we might begin to question His goodness. Knowing this, Jesus told a story to encourage us to keep at it. It begins in Luke with these words: "One day Jesus told his disciples a story to show that they should always pray and never give up" (18:1 NLT).

Jesus told this story because we are all going to have days where we are ready to give up on the miracle we desperately need. He started His story by saying, "There was a judge in a certain city." He didn't say which city, so just pick one; you probably have a judge like this in your own city. Jesus said this particular judge "neither feared God nor cared about people" (v. 2 NLT). We've all experienced someone like this who has way too much power when they should have none.

Jesus told the story of a widow in that city who kept coming to the judge demanding justice. Two thousand years ago, it was difficult for a man to receive justice in a court. It would have been almost impossible for a woman to even be heard! Jesus intentionally picked a widow to show us why we need to pray. The evil judge, who didn't care about justice, finally listened to the woman because, in his words, she was *wearing him out*. Then Jesus said, "Learn a lesson from this unjust judge. Even he rendered a just decision in the end. So don't you think God will surely give justice to his chosen people who cry out to him day and night? Will he keep putting them off?" (vv. 6–7 NLT).

Jesus clearly said that God is more likely to answer prayers repeatedly brought before Him. So listen to Jesus and tell the Lord, "I will bring this before You every day." Why? Because according to Jesus, even an evil judge would answer your request if you kept bringing it. God is supremely good, and as a perfect judge, He will answer your request. So keep bringing your prayer for a miracle day and night.

Why does God want us to come repeatedly before Him? One answer is that it is good for us. We all need to practice prayer. Repetition helps us practice.

FIND YOUR OWN WORDS

When you pray, I encourage you to use your own words. At the end of every chapter, I have written a prayer for you. These are my words. Hopefully as you practice prayer, they become your own words. You need your own words because nothing is more critical to your prayer life than the power that comes from finding your own voice.

Over my years as a pastor, I have been privileged to perform hundreds of wedding ceremonies. When I first started doing weddings, I wasn't very good. I made all kinds of mistakes. On several occasions, I forgot one of the most essential parts: the exchange of rings. One time, after I proudly proclaimed them husband and wife, the wife whispered to me, "You forgot the rings!"

I forgot the rings because I had absolutely no idea what I was doing. So I asked around and got wedding ceremony notes from much older and wiser pastors. That helped immensely. The words and vows were written down. I memorized the notes, and I stopped making so many mistakes. My confidence grew, but I knew something was missing. The ceremonies were beautiful, but they weren't me. So I wrote my own. The previous ones had served to help build my confidence in officiating and praying over a wedding ceremony. That's *exactly* what the formal prayers we learn in church are for. They're the scaffolding on which we build as we learn to talk to God through prayer.

When I started out, people would say, "You screwed that up, Pastor!" (Someone actually said that to me.) But once I changed to my own notes and my own prayers, people responded differently. The truth is, couples don't really care all that much about what the pastor does at the ceremony. They just want to get married.

But when I prayed real prayers I had thought deeply about, and when I talked about real issues I had struggled with myself as a married person, people loved it. They loved it because it was real, and this is the same thing God looks for in our prayers. I have continued to change the way I do weddings. I prefer not to write the vows. I tell the couple, "They are *your* vows, so they should be *your* words." I say this because there is so much power when it's something you believe!

So use my prayers at the end of each chapter. Say them as many times as you like. God will hear you. But what He really longs to hear are the words you feel led to pray. This may feel silly at first, but I encourage you to write out your prayers. Don't you think the widow in Jesus' story had a list of things she wanted the evil judge to hear? So then, write down what it is you want God to hear.

As Jesus contrasted your Father in heaven with the evil judge, notice that the evil judge was bothered by the widow's requests and answered her only because he wanted her to go away. Your Father in heaven will never answer so that you go away. That's the last thing He wants.

He wants you to come to Him for as many miracles as

you need. Remember, He defines Himself as the God who heals.

GOD IS OUR HEALER

Often when God says no, we want to know why—why didn't God heal? But have you ever asked the question, "Why does God heal at all?" Why does God choose to intervene in the natural course of our lives? The answer is, He intervenes and heals because *He is our Healer.* It's who He is. It's how He self-defines.

How do you define yourself? As human beings, we tend to define ourselves by things like race, gender, political party, and so on. When God said, "This is who I am," He said, "I'm your Healer."

When we read the Old Testament, we often can't understand why God's people were doing such unbiblical things. The simple answer is that they didn't yet know God the way they should have. They didn't have the Scriptures like we do. The Israelites we read about in Exodus 15 were in many ways far more Egyptian than Hebrew. This happens to all cultures that move from where they are to someplace new. They were Jews ethnically, but after more than four hundred years of slavery in Egypt, they had become Egyptian culturally.

They'd been there so long, God had to remind them who He had been to them in their past. This is why God reminded Moses that He was the God of Abraham, Isaac, and Jacob. These men were the fathers with whom they once identified. But in many ways they had now forgotten what it meant to be Hebrew. They had to learn about the one true God and put the Egyptian gods out of their minds.

God said, "I will put none of the diseases on you that I put on the Egyptians" (v. 26). Now, you might say, "Wait, wait. God puts diseases on people?" That's what the Bible says. Keep sinning, and it might happen. The Lord put disease after disease on Egypt because Pharaoh kept sinning and wouldn't let God's people go. God told the Hebrews He would not do that to them. He said, in effect, "I want to bless you, and I'm not going to put these diseases on you." His reason? "For I am the LORD,"—wait for it—*your healer*" (v. 26).

Any wound or disease you have is not greater than who God is; He is greater than your problem. He said, "I am the LORD, your healer." In Hebrew, you'd say He is *Jehovah-Rapha*. The Old Testament word translated as "healer" is *rapha*, the one who heals. If you go to the doctor in Israel today, you will see a *rapho*. For thousands of years, the Hebrews went and saw God as their doctor. That's who God is and why we, too, want to go to the Lord for healing.

God has always been a Healer, and the world has long been broken. When Isaiah prophesied about the coming Messiah, he saw Him as a Healer. "But he was pierced for our transgressions, he was crushed for our iniquities; the punishment that brought us peace was on him, and by his wounds we are healed" (Isaiah 53:5 NIV). Isaiah didn't prophesy these words because he hoped they would be true. He knew they were. The world needed healing, so God sent His Messiah, the Christ. Isaiah listed the Messiah's suffering and then its purpose. Jesus did not suffer for no reason. He suffered and died for your healing! Jesus came not just to take away your sins but to bring healing to your soul, mind, and body.

JESUS IS A GOOD DOCTOR

So many people today are afraid to talk to their friends about Jesus. They're afraid to invite their friends to church. Some are ashamed to call themselves Christians. Let me tell you why your friends need Jesus. Let me tell you why Jews, Muslims, and atheists need Jesus.

Because Jesus is a good doctor. He knows what suffering means, and He has the power to heal!

Have you ever been to a doctor's office and felt like he or she didn't hear you? I've had times I felt like, even after I left, they still didn't know why I'd come. Sometimes doctors don't listen like they should because they are human too. But years ago, I had a superhuman experience with an excellent doctor.

I will never forget how the doctor walked in dragging one leg behind him and with one curled arm tucked under his chest. His body seemed partially paralyzed on one side, and he struggled to get through the heavy doors of the hospital. "Hello, Mr. Brown," he said. "Why am I seeing you today?"

I don't remember what my problem was that day, but I will always remember his response. I told him my situation, and he said, "Oh man, I'm so sorry that's happened to you." He hung on to every word I said and responded with, "Hmm, wow." With my insurance plan, I could pick my doctor, and I decided that day to make a change.

On the way out, I told the nurse I wanted him as my primary doctor. She said, "Get in line, honey. Everyone wants him. He is the best."

He really was the best. It wasn't his education; all doctors are highly educated. He was great because he clearly had suffered in his own life. He had been poked, prodded, and wounded, and that made him a great doctor. It's exactly why Jesus did not just come to heal us but to suffer Himself. His suffering made Him an even better Healer. When you come to Jesus with your pain, He listens attentively to your every word and understands how you feel.

> **When you come to Jesus with your pain, He listens attentively to your every word and understands how you feel.**

I don't know if Jesus will heal you, but I know He will hear you. I know if you keep asking, He will answer you. No matter what answer you end up getting, just being in His office will bring some sort of healing. But the only way you will ever experience His miraculous healing power is by asking. Two-thirds of all the miracles Jesus performed were healing miracles. I don't want you to miss out on yours.

Recently a woman came up to me after my sermon and asked for prayer. I could see from her expression that something terrible had happened. She said, "My husband's been in the ICU with COVID, and now he's in a coma. It's grim, and there has been no sign of improvement for days. Would you pray for my husband?" I said I would. We prayed. Her husband came out of the coma just a few days later.

About a week later, I saw her and her husband at church. I screamed, "You got a yes!" She said, "I don't know why." I said, "I don't either, but you got a yes." Just remember that when you are praying, you are praying to a God who *can* say *yes*!

PRAY

Lord Jesus, I know You can do all things. Help me to pray with this confidence, and give me the confidence to find my own voice as I pray. Help me to learn to knock repeatedly, trusting I will get an answer. In Your name, amen.

WATCH

REFLECT

1. How comfortable are you with praying on your own to God?

2. Where do you think you need to grow in finding your own voice as you pray?

3. Are you beginning to see that, as you pray, trusting in what God *can* do will help you grow in faith and confidence?

4. Are there any past disappointments with prayer that are keeping you from praying with faith for your present need?

5. Are you more encouraged or discouraged when you see others receive a powerful yes to their request?

SIX

LEARNING TO WAIT FOR YOUR MIRACLE

I WAITED PATIENTLY FOR THE LORD TO HELP ME,

AND HE TURNED TO ME AND HEARD MY CRY.

PSALM 40:1 NLT

So far, as I have shared with you some of the amazing miracles I have seen God do over the years, I've focused on those that had almost immediate results. These miracles are the exception, not the rule. For most people, when they receive a yes to their miracle, they receive it after waiting. If you find yourself waiting, don't give up. As you will see in this next story, God can still do miracles years after your initial request.

I first met Mitch when he was a teenager. He was on the mountain bike team with my daughters at their high school. He was a great kid. His parents were active in our church, and they seemed to be the perfect family. Mitch was quiet and did not look for attention, but he always got it because he stood head and shoulders above his peers. When he finally stopped growing, he'd reached six foot eight. Mitch was young and handsome and had the world at his fingertips—and then he could not feel them.

After high school, Mitch worked with his dad in construction. With no prior health issues, he began to lose strength in his hands and arms. The weakness moved through his entire body, and he became paralyzed. Day after day, Mitch lay helplessly in a hospital bed, unable to move, waiting for answers. As a young man, he was good at being strong and healthy and struggled when he became weak and sickly. It is not easy to lose control of your body at any age, but for this young man, it was torturous. Every medical test imaginable left doctors with more questions than answers.

Mitch's parents are some of the best supporters of our church and the most exceptional prayer warriors I have ever known. They have spent more time serving the church than some of our paid staff. I knew they prayed for me, so when they asked for prayer for Mitch, I said of course. But after I prayed, he was not healed; he got worse.

His doctor finally suggested a spinal tap. If you don't know what that is, it's a procedure where the doctors place a nine-inch needle into the spine to extract fluid. It is an excruciating process. Mitch told me it was like having a dull nail pushed into his back. The procedure was brutal, but it gave way to a medical answer. Mitch was diagnosed with Guillain-Barré syndrome. Mitch's immune system was attacking the nerves in his body, causing paralysis. This weakness and paralysis can spread to muscles that control breathing, a potentially fatal complication.

The good news was that they had a treatment for his disease. The regimen would require four days in the hospital, with procedures lasting nine hours daily. It was grueling for Mitch, but the treatment was a success. Mitch quickly regained his strength and checked himself out of the hospital on the fourth day after his treatment. He was back at work in just two weeks. It was a medical miracle, or at least we thought so.

In two months, the symptoms returned. Mitch found himself back in the hospital, confused but hopeful a second round of treatment would do the trick. It worked again, but for only a few weeks. The doctors told Mitch and his family there was nothing more they could do at that hospital. He would need to go to a research hospital for further testing.

Mitch and his family kept their faith, believing God would answer their prayers and give Mitch the miracle he desperately needed. However, the results from the research hospital challenged their faith. The doctor delivered unfortunate news: the type of Guillain-Barré syndrome Mitch was experiencing was chronic and, in some rare cases, lifelong. Not the results they were hoping for.

The treatments offered came at significant risk. The

doctors could manage Mitch's current disease, but in time this treatment would invite other problems to his already ravaged body—like leukemia. Mitch chose the risky treatment but did not give up on his miracle. He had praying parents, a praying church, and praying friends, all believing God could do something supernatural.

Mitch's weight plummeted to 130 pounds. He was frail, depressed, confused, and miserable. Why had this happened? Why hadn't God healed him? Though he was discouraged, Mitch faithfully waited for his miracle. In the process, his heart began to change. He quit seeking only a miracle and started to seek God intentionally. As Mitch sought God, he changed careers, surrendered to full-time ministry, and went to Bible college—but still he was not healed.

Mitch suffered from this disease for three long years. He was prayed over at his church, by his Bible college staff, and by his friends, but he did not see any change—until one day he felt led to change his prayer.

For three years, Mitch had faithfully prayed to God, "Please heal me!" Then one night, with a group of Christian friends, he changed his prayer from "Please heal me" to "God, I know You can heal me; I want to know if You are willing to heal me." All through his suffering Mitch had felt God's presence, but this was the first time he heard God's voice.

He heard God say, *I am willing!*

At that moment, Mitch knew God had healed him. I am not suggesting anyone do this, but he was so sure of his miracle that he stopped taking his medicine for a month before telling a soul. Mitch finally told his parents and, even as faithful believers, they were not happy about his decision to abruptly stop his medication. They immediately made an appointment with his specialist. After several tests, his doctor said, "Officially, I cannot tell you that this was a miracle. Still, unofficially, this is a miracle."

Mitch was healed that night he prayed with his friends. He has remained healthy for the last eight years, without a relapse or need for medication. He has regained his strength, weighs over two hundred pounds, loves Jesus, and serves at church. It was officially a miracle. He heard the words *I am willing* and was healed.

Mitch's story is incredible. As I watched him suffer for over three years, I was certain God had said no to our request for a miracle. But God's answer was not no! It was *wait*. Mitch waited patiently for the Lord and got the answer he sought. I cannot guarantee who among us will get the answer we want, but I know we all need to learn to wait on the Lord.

GOD'S TIMING HAS A PURPOSE

Already I have clearly demonstrated that God still heals—over and over again. By now, you know this. But waiting for anything is hard. If you don't believe me, go try waiting for something longer than you think you should.

We all want instant answers. But God is not instant. He is eternal, and He runs on a different clock. The Bible teaches this truth: "A day is like a thousand years to the Lord, and a thousand years is like a day" (2 Peter 3:8 NLT).

Whenever you seek an immediate answer, remember that you are speaking to an eternal God. God does not exist in time but created time so that you and I can exist. It is natural to want God to move faster when you need Him. It is supernatural when you learn to wait patiently for the Lord, and God wants to build the supernatural in you!

God's slowness has a purpose. As you wait for your miracle, consider that there may be more God wants to do than simply to heal you the first time you ask. God is not making you wait to punish you; He is allowing you to wait to empower you.

> God is not making you wait to punish you; He is allowing you to wait to empower you.

Waiting is always an invitation from God to draw you in. You don't just need a miracle; you need God, and waiting forces you to be patient. Pain is an invitation to sit in God's office, waiting for Him. The wait is hard because it feels like a waste of time. But time spent waiting on God is never wasted.

The teaching that it is good to wait on the Lord comes from an important but often unread book: the book of Lamentations. I wish we could rename the book "Uh-oh," because I think more people would read it. To *lament* means to process grief and sorrow. For the Israelites, this was a book of reflection on what had gone wrong. They were processing the loss of their capital and the destruction of their people. In Hebrew, Lamentations is the book of "How?" As in, How did this happen? In the next chapter we will deal with handling the "how" when God says no.

Lamenting is a way of organizing our thoughts and putting our emotions to paper. While waiting on your miracle, you will have more time to think than you want. Don't waste this process. Write down what you are feeling! God is working in this—for your benefit. Take lots of notes, because there are always things to learn while you wait for your answer.

WAITING HELPS US LEARN

My grandmother Junella was an extraordinary woman who took me to church when I was young. I went to Sunday school with her, and she taught me many things about God. However, on her deathbed, she said, "Why won't God just take me home? What does God want me to learn?"

It's bizarre to offer your grandmother spiritual wisdom. "Grandma," I said, "the lesson is, you're not God. We don't get to decide when it's our time. God is still God even when you are ninety-one." That's a lot of years to us, but it is nothing compared to eternity. No matter how old we are or how long we've been a Christian, there is always something to learn as we wait on the Lord.

Time spent in class seemed like forever when we were young, right? Jesus was called Rabbi by almost everyone who knew Him. *Rabbi* means teacher. As a follower of Jesus, class is always in session. The suffering you are enduring will not last forever, but the lessons you learn will.

One lesson the Lord wants to teach you is that He is willing to risk lives to save souls. He always has been, and He always will be. This is what Peter was trying to teach us about God's purposeful slowness when he said, "A thousand years are like a day" (2 Peter 3:8 NIV). God doesn't just want to heal you; He wants you to *know* Him. It takes time to know Him, and waiting is a way to allow for this time.

Waiting for our miracle is one of the ways we learn to become entirely dependent on Him. I don't know what situation you are facing or what pain you are going through as you read this, but I know where I was.

After injuring my back at the gym, I was stuck writing this chapter for weeks.

My body is fifty-one, but my brain too often insists that I am still fifteen! In the gym, they call what I did "ego lifting." It's where an old guy tries to prove he's still got it. The only thing I proved was that I can still be ridiculously foolish. I hurt my back doing something I knew I should not have done.

If you have ever experienced back issues, you know the pain I went through. If not, imagine what it might feel like to be stabbed in the back. Only the knife is ice-cold, and it puts out an electric charge that shocks you from your mid-back to your lower body and into your toes. Any movement drops you helplessly to the floor, writhing in pain.

I couldn't stand. Couldn't sit. Couldn't read. And couldn't write.

I went to the doctor, a physical therapist, and a chiropractor—and I got worse. The drugs made me feel stoned and dulled the pain only slightly.

It took me about ten days to break. As I was working

through this chapter, a fellow pastor who knew I was writing about waiting pointed out what my pain was allowing me to miss. When pain shouts, God whispers! God wanted me to write about waiting while I was in the midst of waiting.

Everyone has a different schedule for when they finally break down. Ten days of being completely dependent on others was my limit. Ten days for me to remember what I knew all along: I can't do anything without God.

Health gives us the illusion that we are strong and independent. Pain reveals the honest truth: we are not. I didn't just need to write a chapter on waiting. God needed to write it once again on my soul. So as I wrote this, I waited. I didn't want to, but I am not God. So I've learned to wait . . . *again*.

WAITING STRENGTHENS OUR CHARACTER

Waiting is a way God marks you with His character. It is a way He makes you better. Instant healing will relieve your suffering, but it may do nothing to conform you into Christlikeness.

In Luke 17, we see a prime example of how an instant miracle can heal a body but not affect character. On His way to Jerusalem, Jesus found ten men sick with leprosy. Leprosy is a terrible disease that causes severe, disfiguring skin sores and nerve damage. For millennia, people with this

> **Waiting is a way God marks you with His character. It is a way He makes you better.**

disease had to isolate themselves from their friends and family because it was contagious.

The people with leprosy in Luke 17 were from different ethnic and religious backgrounds. Brought together because of their illness, they begged for pity from Jesus, knowing this painful disease was a slow death sentence. With a simple command, Jesus sent them away, directing them to go and show themselves to a priest.

In those days, priests also operated as de facto doctors regarding public health. If you got a certificate from the priest declaring that you were well, you could return to your former life. Knowing that Jesus was a powerful miracle worker, these ten men hustled off expectantly to see the priest. On their way, one of the ten noticed he was completely healed. He immediately returned to Jesus, thanking Him and praising God.

Jesus asked, "Were not all ten cleansed? Where are the other nine? Has no one returned to give praise to God except this foreigner?" (vv. 17–18 NIV).

What Jesus said is amazing and important. You see, Jesus healed all ten lepers. But only one had a change of heart. Think about that. Nine out of the ten who received an instant miracle did not return to thank Jesus for what they begged Him to do. Why? Because miracles are not nearly as powerful as waiting is to bring about the character change we need!

Jesus turned to the man and said, "Rise and go; your faith has made you well" (v. 19 NIV). All ten men were healed. But only one man was made well.

As we discussed earlier, Jesus came both to save and to

heal. Remember, the Greek word *sozo* can be translated as either "save" or "heal." Can you guess what Greek word is translated as "well" in verse 19 to describe the second miracle? If you guessed *sozo*, you are correct. Jesus wants to heal all of you. Not just the parts you think need to be made right, but all of your parts that only *He* can make right.

Jesus healed all ten lepers, but only one was healed inside and out—the Samaritan who returned to say thanks. God wants a better return on His miracles than 10 percent. So He allows us to wait for Him. Not just so that we are ready to be healed but so that, in our waiting, we are ready to be changed.

LEARNING TO WAIT

Nothing changes us faster than waiting! That last sentence is kind of a play on words, but it's true. Instant everything ruins us.

In the book *Charlie and the Chocolate Factory* by Roald Dahl, Veruca Salt is one of the most hated characters. She continually says, "I want it now, Daddy!" In the story, her father gave her everything she ever wanted the moment she asked for it. Veruca and her father ultimately both end up in a furnace. *Charlie and the Chocolate Factory* shows us what happens when a father gives in to his child's every wish. You end up in hell on earth!

Your Father in heaven loves you too much to give you everything you ask for every time you ask for it. He makes you wait to make you better.

Some of the best characters in the Bible had to learn to wait. Noah was one of the first. He had to wait to build a boat. He had to wait for the animals to get on the boat. He had to wait for rain. He had to wait for the rain to stop. He had to wait for the water to recede. He had to wait for a dove to return. He had to wait for the boat to rest on land. Noah was not just a boatbuilder; he was a professional waiter!

In Hebrew, the word translated as "wait" can be translated another way—"hope"! You see, most people lose hope as time passes. God wants you to learn to find it.

Noah was not the only character in the Bible who had to wait. Abraham had to wait for a child. When his wife heard an angel say that she would get pregnant at ninety, she laughed. She had a baby nine months later and named him Isaac, which in Hebrew means "laughter"! She waited her entire life, and only when she had given up all hope of being a mom was she finally ready to be one. You see, it was the waiting that changed her, and your waiting is changing you!

I don't know what miracle you are waiting for. So many people I've prayed with are tired of the not knowing; they just need a word from God. You might say, "I'm not looking for land, and I don't need a baby; I just need a word from God today."

Did you know that Moses had to wait for the Ten Commandments? They took *time*. God didn't send them by email or text. Moses had to wait for some of the most powerful words in human history, and we need to learn to wait for ours. The Lord said to Moses, "Come up to me on the mountain and wait there" (Exodus 24:12).

God will answer when you are ready. God allows us to wait so that we have the strength to handle whatever answer He gives. You *will* get a response from God—either yes, no, or wait.

WHILE WE'RE WAITING, GOD IS WORKING

While we wait, we may feel like nothing is happening. Just know, God is working while you are waiting. Just because you can't see what God is currently doing does not mean He is doing nothing. God may have called *you* to be still, but that does not mean He is still.

The apostle Paul wrote, "We know that in all things God works for the good of those who love him, who have been called according to his purpose" (Romans 8:28 NIV). God is *actively* working amid your situation. No matter what it is and no matter how bad it is, God works *all* things for good in your life. So the question is never "Is God working?" but rather "How and where is God working?" And the answer is always the same.

Most Christians memorize Romans 8:28 but never think about the next verse, which says that God is working to make us "conformed to the image of his Son" (v. 29 NIV). Christianity is not about being instantly fixed but about being eternally transformed. This takes more time sitting with our suffering than we would like. The longer we faithfully wait in it, the more like Jesus we become. Jesus was dependent on God for everything, and we should be too.

When we are young and healthy, we depend primarily on ourselves. But when we are injured, aged, or battling a disease or situation beyond our strength, we learn to become fully dependent on God. His work isn't to allow you to avoid all suffering and pain. God allows suffering and pain to make you more like Jesus.

Keep waiting and keep trusting. The Bible says, "The LORD is good to those who wait for him" (Lamentations 3:25). I don't want to miss out on His goodness, as so many people do!

WAITING IS GOOD FOR US

In my midthirties, I had LASIK surgery on my eyes. In pre-op, the nurse said I would have surgery on two different tables. The first table was where the surgeon would use a scalpel to cut my lenses. Then I would move to a second table where the surgeon would use a laser to fix my eyesight. As if this wasn't scary enough, the nurse explained that I would be temporarily blind.

She tried to reassure me—I would be blind only for a few minutes and needn't worry because they would give me enough Xanax to relax me. Well, I *wasn't* relaxed. Surgery is never fun. But to be awake for the entire procedure was scary!

As I lay on the first table, the surgeon came in and said, "When I cut your eyes, you will be temporarily blind." He said not to worry and that he would be there the entire time. I was reassured—until I realized I could not see at all.

I wasn't kind of blind; I was totally blind! When I started to panic, the doctor said, "You're going to have to trust me."

That's easy when you are reading the brochure. It's not so easy when you realize you can't see at all. Next the nurse told me to stick out my hands, and I did. She grabbed them and said, "I won't let go." She said this was the hardest part.

"What part?" I said.

"The trusting part!" she said. Holding my hands, she led me. "I'm still here," she would say. "You're going to be okay."

Then they put me on another table, and the doctor said, "I'm here. You're going to be okay. After this is over, you will see better than you ever have before." I don't know if my doctor and nurse were Christians, but they were preaching that day! In my mind, I was going to be *sort of* blind for a few minutes. Instead I was *completely* blind for a few hours. And terrified the entire time.

Trusting when you can't see is the hardest thing to do. It's one thing to know about waiting conceptually. It's another thing to be in it, hurting, afraid, and trusting someone you cannot see.

Waiting on the Lord is good for us, *especially* when we cannot see Him. Waiting teaches us to look for the Lord with our souls and not just with our sight. Waiting teaches us to hear His voice and trust His goodness.

While you wait, lift up your hands. Jesus, the surgeon, is right there. Even though you can't see Him, He hasn't left you. He's right there. His angels are your nurses,

> **Waiting teaches us to look for the Lord with our souls and not just with our sight.**

ensuring you are held and guided. You don't know what Jesus will do, but you know what He will never do: He will never let you go!

While you are waiting, He is working to make you more trusting. More like Him. Waiting is so hard, but it is also a tool God uses to help us truly see.

PRAY

Lord Jesus, help me to be still. Please help me to wait. Help me to want You more than my miracle. I know that in my waiting, You are working. Help me to feel Your presence and Your strength. Help me to trust You as You work. I pray this in Your name, amen.

WATCH

REFLECT

1. How do you typically respond when you have to wait?
2. What might God be teaching you as you wait?
3. How can you grow in your relationship with God as you wait?
4. What wisdom have you learned from waiting that you can share with others?
5. How do you need to be prayed for as you wait?

SEVEN

WHEN GOD SAYS NO TO A MIRACLE

THREE DIFFERENT TIMES I BEGGED THE LORD TO TAKE IT AWAY. EACH TIME HE SAID, "MY GRACE IS ALL YOU NEED. MY POWER WORKS BEST IN WEAKNESS."

2 CORINTHIANS 12:8-9 NLT

Trigger warning: This chapter includes the stories of individuals who chose to end their lives, including a child. If you are struggling with suicidal thoughts, please call or text the Suicide and Crisis Lifeline at 988 or reach out to a trusted pastor or licensed mental health professional for help. God has a plan for your life!

God will answer *every* prayer. Sometimes God, in His mercy, says yes to our need for a miracle. Sometimes God says wait, for our benefit. Sometimes God says no.

Nothing is more difficult than getting a firm no after you have made a desperate plea for a yes.

As a pastor, I have had the privilege to rejoice with people when God said yes. I have had to grow in patience as I've sat with people when God said wait. I have also had the burden of grieving with people when God said no.

The most heart-wrenching no I have ever had to process came after a miraculous yes. The yes came with two of my dearest friends. They have faithfully served with me in ministry for almost twenty years. Andrew and Rebecca are an amazing couple and incredible friends. We work together and have met together in small group. Everything was great in their marriage until they decided it was time to have children. Like many couples, they struggled with fertility. Both my wife and I sat with them as they processed, prayed, and trusted God through this difficult time. As it became clear that having a biological child was unlikely, God began to put the idea of adoption in their hearts.

Our leadership team attended a conference where one of the speakers challenged the audience to consider adoption. The invitation at the end of the talk was clear and straightforward. The woman speaking asked people to stand if the Lord was calling them to open their hearts to adopt a child. Andrew and Rebecca both stood. I will never forget it. It was a powerful God moment for sure.

I would love to tell you that the adoption process was easy and smooth, but it wasn't. It was awful, expensive, and discouraging. My friends felt led to adopt from Ethiopia. There was paperwork and one setback after another, and always more money required.

After several years of this painstakingly slow process, we held a prayer night for their adoption. But right before the prayer night began, Ethiopia announced that no more adoptions would be allowed unless you were Ethiopian. My friends were devastated. It wasn't right, it didn't seem fair, and all hope seemed lost. They felt God had clearly said no to a biological child and now wondered if He was saying no to adoption.

We met with our dear friends that night and watched them cry out to God. The room was filled with grief and doubt and tons of questions. Person after person prayed over them and spoke encouraging words to them. Then God spoke to me. What God said shocked me. But I knew it was God, so I spoke it to them. I said, "What makes you think God needs an open Ethiopia to bring you your Ethiopian child?"

The room was silent. What I said had either been God's words or incredibly insensitive. The room was quiet, but I was not. I knew I had heard from God. Ethiopia was closed, but God had opened their heart to Ethiopia for a reason. That night in prayer, we called upon God, and in just a few weeks they would answer a phone call confirming what I heard.

The call was about a five(ish)-year-old- boy who had been adopted from Ethiopia. It wasn't working out with his current adoptive family, and he would need a new one. I say "ish" because many adopted children don't know their age, so you're often left to guess. I have other good friends with an adopted son who turned "six" on his birthday three years in a row. Orphanages will often do this because the younger the child, the easier it is to place them with a family.

They met with their new young son. He was handsome and very quiet. Andrew and Rebecca were his fourth set of guardians, but he was finally in his forever home. Sometime later, God brought them another son under the same circumstances: a previous adoption that didn't work out. His name was Nobel. God had answered their prayers and given them a yes, twice, and they were a family.

As Christians, we are all adopted. God has only one biological Son, and His name is Jesus. Adoption is a beautiful thing. But for anyone considering it, it is extremely challenging. Both boys struggled. The orphanages that raised these boys are led by wonderful, well-meaning people. But there are often way too many kids and not enough supervising adults. Children are not held enough or protected. They have to learn to fend for themselves and are often subjected to pain by older children who have also been raised without their needs being met. At times, these older kids turn into abusers. On top of that, both boys had been brought to a new country and placed with families where it ultimately didn't work out. The boys had lots of wounds and lots of doubts about the reliability of adults.

Because adults had failed them so many times, my friends' children had a hard time trusting anyone. They struggled to bond and attach to their new parents and had difficulty receiving and showing love. It wasn't their fault. They hadn't received love while developing those relational skills as babies and then as toddlers.

One of their sons struggled but was progressing, and the other son, Nobel, got worse. He had seen more pain and experienced more rejection in his short life. He was beautiful on the outside but deeply broken on the inside. No matter what my friends tried, he grew more angry and, at times, violent. He struggled in school and was defiant and difficult. Every day was a battle with his parents over the simplest tasks. There were moments when he was scary.

Nobel wasn't always in a troubled state. He had an incredible sense of humor. He was one of the most athletically gifted kids I have ever seen for his age. He had one of the best friends a kid could ask for and spent a lot of time with his friend's family. Nobel loved adventure, especially at church camp. He thrived when things were great, but he crumbled when things did not go his way.

One January, things began to not go his way. We were all aware of his struggles with behavior on the outside, but no one knew how much he was tormented on the inside. He had been meeting with a counselor and seemed to connect well with him. But things at school had grown so bad the school decided to make a change and move him to a new classroom. A simple change like that would be a fairly small, uneventful transition for you and me. But for Nobel, any change was a trigger for his pain, fear of abandonment, and fear of rejection. Unbeknownst to anyone in his life, on that January morning, he just couldn't take another change.

At the age of twelve, Nobel made an irreversible decision to hurt himself. My dear friend found his son slumped over in the shower. Nobel was not breathing and had no pulse. An ambulance rushed him to the hospital. Tammy and I rushed to meet them. When we arrived, the hospital was chaotic. It is the region's trauma center, where the most severe cases are brought for care. The waiting room was full of hurting people, as well as family and friends of those who had suffered inexplicable trauma.

When we made our way to the small curtain-lined area in the ER, Nobel was lying on a gurney surrounded by his loving mother and father. All the family's pastors and their wives were there as well. Loud machines, mimicking inhales and exhales and beeping out of sync, were breathing for him. I couldn't get past the fact that, even with all the tubes running in and out of him, he was still so beautiful—even his hair was perfectly in place. His body was motionless except when the machine forced air into his lungs, causing his muscles to ripple—for an instant. I thought, *If anyone can come back from this, Nobel can.*

We all prayed in faith, believing God could heal. We knew that God was a God of miracles because Nobel's very presence in our lives was testimony to this fact. We pleaded with God for healing in Jesus' name, but it was not meant to be. After what seemed like hours but was mere minutes, a team of doctors came in and said that Nobel's brain showed no activity. It took his body a couple of days to confirm the devastating reality that he was not coming back home.

I don't know why, but my wife and I had ended up on separate sides of Nobel's hospital bed. When the gut-wrenching words left the doctor's lips, I watched my dear friend Andrew collapse in pain across from me. I can still see his fingers intensely gripping the sheets in clenched fists as he fell to the floor.

I quickly turned to his wife, who was standing next to me, her eyes wide in momentary disbelief. I could only whisper the words, "I'm sorry," before she fell into my arms.

I held Rebecca. My wife tried unsuccessfully to lift Andrew. The entire room—full of people believing in a miracle—was in shock.

God said *no*!

This was the most difficult no for me to comprehend. The no was excruciating because there were *so many* yeses for Andrew and Rebecca even to *have* Nobel as their son. God had spoken *so powerfully* to them at the conference. And God had spoken *so clearly* to us in a small group. Why would God do all these wonderful things, only to say no when we needed Him the most?

ASKING GOD WHY?

When we get a clear no, "why?" is the most honest question we can ask. We shouldn't feel bad about our questions; Jesus asked the same thing just before He died.

> And about the ninth hour Jesus cried out with a loud voice, saying, "Eli, Eli, lema sabachthani?" that is, "My God, my God, why have you forsaken me?" (Matthew 27:46)

This is one of the most powerful verses in Scripture. It is one of the most important verses for those who get a clear no to their request for a miracle.

I want you to notice something important. Jesus, the Son of God, cried out to His own Father, "Why?" His request was so raw and real that Bible authors have left what He said in the language in which He said it. Jesus wanted to know why

God said no! However, what Jesus said here was more than just His words in that moment—He was quoting Psalm 22:

> My God, my God, why have you forsaken me?
>   Why are you so far from saving me, from the words
> of my groaning? (v. 1).

Psalm 22 illustrates the many things that Jesus would go through. But it is also where you see something we all go through at some point. There will be a time in your life when God disappoints you. You will feel abandoned by Him when you need Him the most—and you will want to know why.

It's okay to ask why.

It's okay to ask why. We desire answers to make sense of our pain. It gets dangerous when we come up with answers on our own.

So often we think of the crucifixion, with Jesus lifted up high on a hill. But Romans did not push the condemned up and away from sight. They crucified people on the most trafficked spots so that everyone, especially Rome's enemies, saw what happened to those who messed with Roman power. The cross of Christ was low to the ground. His feet would have been just above the dirt. Rome wanted the condemned at eye level.

Jesus' suffering was unavoidable for those who passed by. Bystanders didn't know what to do when Jesus cried out in agony that God had abandoned Him. They were getting their groceries before the Passover holiday. As they exited the city, they noticed Jesus suffering on the roadside.

They couldn't avoid Him; they couldn't go around Him. They would have been able to look into Jesus' eyes as He screamed for God. Some did what we all might do. They thought what many of us would have thought; after all, we must do *something*.

So they offered Jesus wine. Not good wine but sour wine. Often when we try to put a bow on someone's suffering or try to help, we end up offering sour wine or words that sour the soul.

I have heard people who intend to be helpful say things like, "God must have needed a beautiful flower for His garden in heaven, and that's why He took your mom." Grief causes us to do and say senseless things. When we say things like this, we make God the cause of someone's suffering. God is not the cause—sin is. Jesus did not die on that cross to bring you pain but to alleviate it forever. He will help you with some of your pain in this life and all of it in the next.

As you process your grief and pain, notice something in the text that you may have missed. Jesus did *not* get an answer to the *most* painful question He ever asked. Jesus needed an answer to His question of why, but His answer was silence. There is always more to grief and sadness than we will understand on this side of heaven.

ASKING GOD HOW?

We may or may not get all of our questions answered in heaven. We don't yet know what that process will be like. What we do know is that we have to figure out how to move forward on earth. Whatever your loss, whatever your pain, the better question is "How?"

My humble suggestion as you process your pain is that instead of asking God why, ask Him how. This subtle change has helped me through some of my greatest pain.

As we discussed in the previous chapter, the original name of the book of Lamentations is "How?" This approach is so helpful as we grieve. It's why God put a book in the Bible called "How?"—to help grieving people process our suffering and loss.

As you process your grief, ask God "how" questions. Try asking, "How on earth am I going to get through this?" As Jesus prepared to suffer on the cross, before He asked why, He asked God if there was any other way. Jesus knew what He was facing. Death is never easy, even for the Son of God. So He asked, just as He's teaching us to ask.

> [Jesus] fell on his face and prayed, saying, "My Father, if it be possible, let this cup pass from me; nevertheless, not as I will, but as you will." (Matthew 26:39)

Jesus was praying for the same reason you and I should: *prayer can change reality*. Miracles are interventions by God into the way things are.

Sweating drops of blood, Jesus asked God to intervene because He *knew* what God could do. This prayer was no formality. It was real, it was raw, and it was right for Jesus to ask. Suffering may have to be accepted, but it should never be celebrated.

Jesus asked for a miracle, and God said no. If God can

say no to Jesus, He can and will say no to you and me. God will not say yes to every miracle you pray for. God will not allow you to avoid all suffering, but He will *never* ask you to suffer alone.

How will you get through what you know you can't?

How will you navigate hell on earth?

These are the better questions. And the answer is *with the power of heaven.*

HELP FROM HEAVEN

Whenever God says no to a miracle of healing, He instantly says yes to a miracle of strength. Jesus asked God three times to save Him from His horrible death, and three times God said no. A no from God is never easy, and that's why Jesus will never make you go through it with only your own strength. In Luke's gospel, he added a beautiful verse that I hope will help you with asking God "How?" as you process your no.

Immediately following the no, Jesus received from God the strength to carry on.

And there appeared to him an angel from heaven, strengthening him. (Luke 22:43)

If Jesus needed strength from heaven when He received a no from God, so will you. We will all face more in this life than we can handle. Jesus thought He couldn't handle the cross, but with strength from heaven, He did. As you suffer the pain and the loss from your "no" on earth, look for your strength from heaven. When He wants to send you strength, God will often send an angel. But angels are not always easy to identify.

There is an amazing book in the Bible called the Letter to the Hebrews—Hebrews for short. You're probably not supposed to have a favorite book in the Bible, but if I had one, it would be Hebrews. There is so much theology, practical advice, and direction in this book. I love it. And there's an incredible truth tucked within its pages regarding angels. It says, "Don't forget to show hospitality to strangers, for some who have done this have entertained angels without realizing it!" (13:2 NLT).

Don't be too quick to say you have never seen an angel. They are all around us, sent by God to strengthen His children when they get a no to their prayers, no matter how large or small that prayer is. All prayers are all-important to God.

I believe I met my first angel when I was fourteen. It was at a Little League game in Sacramento, California, in 1986. Greg LeMond was a local celebrity, having become the first American to win the Tour de France. In an instant, many kids went from wanting to be professional skateboarders to wanting to be the next Greg LeMond. I was one of those kids. The problem was that a decent ten-speed bike was hundreds, if not thousands, of dollars more than the best skateboard. It was simply not in my parents' price range.

I had wonderful, generous parents and was blessed to have a great dad. Every other week he would take me out on a father-son date. I took him to the local bicycle store. I showed him all the bikes, and we talked about Greg

LeMond, the Tour de France, and so many of my dreams. He asked which bike I liked. He had no idea how much they cost, so I showed him a bike that was blue and silver, a Nishiki International. Nishiki is now called Giant Bicycles, and that was probably my dad's first thought as he looked at the enormous price tag!

Up to that point, I had never seen my dad cry. He was a man of emotion but not of tears. He was so excited, and I could feel his energy matching mine as we shopped—until he saw the price tag. He stepped back, dropped his head in shame, and said, "Son, there is just no way."

Instantly, I felt terrible. I never wanted to make my father feel that way. He was a wonderful dad, but we were the working poor. We drove home in silence, and I made a promise to God as I prayed that I would never, and I mean never, ask my dad for that bike again.

Until the very next day.

I enjoyed baseball, but I wasn't very good. Weekly, I sat on the bench as my team took the field. On a particular day as I was riding the bench, a young man pulled up on a brand-new, shiny ten-speed. It was a blue and silver Nishiki International, exactly like the one in the store. Because I was the only one sitting there, he looked at me and said, "Hey, kid, you want to buy a bike?"

Without even thinking, I said, "Yeah, how much?"

He said, "Seventy-five bucks!" I asked if the bike was stolen; he laughed and told me it wasn't.

I ran out of the dugout, passed my coach, and found my parents. I told my dad about the bike, and he shook his head in disbelief and said, "Let's take a look." The bike looked like it had never been ridden. The young man said he was in the air force and had just bought it, but he was being shipped out to Guam the next day and couldn't take it with him. He assured my dad it wasn't stolen. My dad asked how much, and when the man said it was seventy-five bucks, my dad, who was a pastor, said, "That's weird. I got paid an extra seventy-five dollars for a wedding this week." So we bought it!

I was ecstatic; my mom was not! She was certain it was stolen.

My mom is a rule follower, so she made me take my blue-and-silver bike to the police station. They had no reports of a bike matching that description being stolen. Then she made me go to the bike store. They had no record of the bike. The bike store even called Nishiki's corporate office, and they had no record of the serial number imprinted on the bike frame. They said it was a Nishiki, for sure. It was brand-new and in perfect condition, but they had no idea how or where it was made. The Nishiki representative said, "We don't know where it is from, but it came from somewhere, just not from us!" I believe it was an angel, who strengthened the faith of a young man and the faith of a small-church pastor.

The bicycle hangs in my church office to this day to remind me that angels are all around, strengthening us and ministering to us.

You are not alone. You don't have to go through this alone. God is with you, and His strength is with you. So how are you going to get through this? The answer is, not with your strength but with all the flex heaven offers. It's why the apostle Paul said, "I can do everything through Christ, who gives me strength" (Philippians 4:13 NLT). You have got this because Christ has got you!

It has been a few years since Nobel's passing. They have been long, hard years. My friends lost a beloved son but found supernatural strength. There were angels in the emergency room that day. They held Andrew and Rebecca when they could not stand and loved them as they questioned God's love for them. Some of those angels were from heaven, and some were ordinary friends—angels on earth. Friends who cried and stood with them as they found their heavenly strength—a strength stronger than pain that finds hope even in the face of death.

DEATH DOES NOT HAVE THE LAST WORD

The next answer to how you will get through your no is that death does not have the last word; Jesus does. Every no on earth for healing will be a yes in heaven if you know Jesus. On earth, you may receive a "no," but eternally speaking, you just got a "wait!"

Nobel was too young and impulsive to fully comprehend what he did to himself. I never questioned his salvation. I *knew* that no love on earth could heal what life on earth had done to his precious heart. I knew he was with God. I knew that he had been saved.

But I had another friend I was not so sure about. His name was Stephen. He was a young, healthy, and successful man in his late twenties. He was older and wiser than Nobel and should have known better than to take his own life. His whole life was laid out ahead of him—so much so that he was getting married in a few weeks. I was at someone else's wedding rehearsal when I got a call from his father, who said in distress, "Stephen is dead. Please come as quickly as you can." I left immediately, knowing what I'd heard but in disbelief. I thought, *Stephen can't be dead; he's getting married*. But he was dead, and he had taken his own life.

Stephen's dad was one of my best friends. He grew up Irish Methodist, which meant that suicide, to him, was a gravely immoral act, thought to be an unforgivable sin. When I arrived at Stephen's house, his panicked father's first question was, "Is Stephen in heaven or hell?"

I wasn't ready for the chaos that surrounded death from suicide. The police were investigating, the fire department was taking a report, and grieving family and friends were making their way to the house that was supposed to be preparing for a wedding, realizing they would now be preparing for a funeral. It was awful.

I wasn't ready for my friend's question, so I answered honestly. "I don't know." I thought I knew Stephen, but I realized I didn't. Behind his smiles were fears, depression, and anxiety that he had kept hidden from us. I was wrecked by this question and thought about it constantly for the next few days. I honestly didn't know whether Stephen was with God or the alternative.

I didn't sleep much leading up to Stephen's funeral. The

night before the service, I went to bed early and was sound asleep. I was awakened suddenly with a vision in the middle of the night. My room was filled with an extraordinary bright light. For a moment I wasn't sure if it was a police raid or an alien abduction—but it was the most magnificent light I had ever seen.

The corners of my bedroom began to be stretched outward, almost like dropping a bowling ball in a grocery store shopping bag. The walls looked like heated, melting rubber as they moved to accommodate something much larger than the room and abundantly more powerful. I was terrified. I sat up and rubbed my eyes in disbelief. I thought I must be dreaming, but I had never been more awake.

In the middle of the light in the corner, a figure reclined on some sort of throne. The figure moved like light shining through rippling water. The figure was totally relaxed, while I had never been more stressed. The figure held a scepter in His right hand. The scepter was longer than I thought it should be. It looked heavy, but the figure held it effortlessly. He said in a voice that bellowed and shook me to my soul, *Do not be afraid.* Let me tell you, I was!

The figure then said, *Stephen is with Me; he is with Us!* It was as if He spoke both in the singular and plural tense at the same time. He moved closer toward me and said, *He is with Me; he is with Us.* The room grew still. I don't know how long I sat there motionless, but time seemed to disappear. I didn't know what to say, and I don't think I would have been able to form words if I wanted to.

I could see my wife sleeping peacefully next to me. I wanted to scream at her to wake up but was afraid. I looked back at the figure, and He said, *Go to sleep.* I said, "Okay," and I did.

The next day I spoke at Stephen's funeral. I told his father about my vision. He cried and said thank you. Then he asked me, why had the Lord not appeared to him? Without even thinking about it, I said, "Because you wouldn't have believed your dream, and God knew you would believe mine."

I know Stephen is alive and in heaven. Not because of what he did or didn't do. He is in heaven because of what Jesus did. Jesus died and rose on the third day so you could live forever with Him. In Christ, everyone is healed. We all experience *sozo* forever. We will all eventually be healed on the inside and out. I am so sorry if you got a no to your prayer, but one day because of Jesus, it *will* be a yes. Jesus will make all things new!

No more tears, no more death, and no more nos.

PRAY

Lord Jesus, help me to move from a "Why?" to a "How?" Please send me Your strongest angels to strengthen me. Help me to trust in the reality of heaven and the hope of resurrection! I pray this in Your name, amen.

WATCH

REFLECT

1. Describe the most painful no you have ever received to prayer.
2. You may never know why you received a no. How might changing your question from "Why?" to "How?" help you?
3. Whenever the Lord says no to our prayers, He instantly gives a yes to His strength. As you process your no, where have you seen God's strength?
4. Angels are all around, ministering to us when we need strength. What can you do to be more aware of this gift from heaven?
5. How can the reality of the resurrection give you hope that the no you receive will be a yes when Jesus returns?

EIGHT

DISCOVERING GOD'S WILL FOR YOUR MIRACLE

THEREFORE DO NOT BE FOOLISH, BUT UNDERSTAND WHAT THE WILL OF THE LORD IS.

EPHESIANS 5:17

I sat down with a young pastor who shared his incredible journey of discovering God's will as he and his wife cried out for a miracle from God Almighty. As a couple, they'd been thrilled to find out they were pregnant. As they began to plan for their growing family, they set an appointment to get a routine ultrasound. Ultrasounds are a wonderful gift from science. With technology, we can see what once only God could see—babies being formed in the darkness of their mother's womb. Technology creates wonderful miracles from modern science and difficult moral decisions for those who live in a contemporary world. This pastor and his wife looked forward to seeing one of the first images of the newest member of their family.

The sonographer engaged in casual conversation with the excited but nervous couple. At the same time, she captured pictures from the ultrasound as she identified key parts of the new child's anatomy. The room was full of joy and expectation. Then the sonographer became silent. The silence was instantly concerning, but the parents were left with their own thoughts until, finally, the silence was broken. "I need to get the radiologist," the sonographer said stoically. She left the room, and the parents' hearts sank.

A few moments later, a doctor entered the room and looked at the radiology report—specifically, the area in question. The problem was the child's brain. Something was missing in it, something important. The doctor explained that the child was missing the corpus callosum, a major part of the brain that ensures both sides of the brain can communicate with each other. Without it, their child would potentially struggle in life and could have other major complications. The child might never walk or talk and could have multiple cognitive challenges. Ultimately, the doctor explained, the child might not survive delivery. The doctor asked if they would like to speak further about their options regarding the pregnancy.

My young friend and his wife were devastated, but they knew what they needed to do. They needed a miracle. They had no idea what God would do, but they believed whole-heartedly in what God *could* do.

They would be in for a rough ride. There was no way to know the full extent of the problem until the child could get an MRI one week after being born. They were on a journey where they regularly cried out to God for the miracle they needed for their baby boy. They believed God heard their cries as they sought His will.

It's easier to believe that God can heal than wait and see if He *will* heal. We know what God *can* do, but we seldom know what He *will* do regarding the miraculous. The Gospel of Matthew offers the perfect road map to discovering God's will for your miracle. No matter what you are praying through, this road map will help guide you as you pray.

A ROAD MAP FOR DISCOVERING GOD'S WILL

In Matthew 8, Jesus encountered a man suffering from leprosy. This horrible disease had isolated this man from his family and friends and threatened his life. The man was desperate for a miracle and believed Jesus could do one.

Suddenly, a man with leprosy approached [Jesus] and knelt before him. "Lord," the man said, "if you are willing, you can heal me and make me clean." (v. 2 NLT)

Before we ask God for a miracle, we must understand the meaning of a miracle. *A miracle is God intervening in your or someone else's life to change the present circumstances.* We are asking God to change the very fabric of reality. So when we need a miracle of this magnitude to confront a massive problem in our lives, we must begin by reminding ourselves of the immense power of God.

Notice that when the man approached Jesus, he said, "If you are willing, you can heal me." This is such amazing faith from someone who had suffered so much. He approached Jesus not because of what he knew Jesus would do but because he believed in what Jesus *could* do. The man knew he was asking for something supernatural, but he also believed he was asking someone with supernatural power!

When you or I are *overwhelmed* with life, it is most likely because we have become *underwhelmed* with God. God is always bigger than what we know. Even for all eternity, we will be wowed each day by something new we learned about God. If we have spent years studying God, there is still more to Him than we know. I have spent the last twenty-five years learning about God. Someone recently asked me what that was like. I responded, "It's like trying to empty the ocean with a coffee cup. You can scoop every day of your life and never even come close to its depth."

There is more to God than you know. This journey is not just for your miracle, and it's not just about the healing you need. It's about the depths of the Healer you need to know. The Healer is all-powerful! So enjoy this journey. Don't be afraid to be a beginner. Your confidence should not come from your ability to pray but from God's ability to change your situation. You don't know what God will do, but if you want to see a miracle, believe in what He *can* do. Take the first step.

Trust in What God Can Do

The first step on your journey to understand God's will is to trust in what He can do. That's what the man with leprosy did, and that's what you and I must do. We don't have to believe in the outcome, but we must believe in the One who can miraculously change our outcome.

Ask God for What You Want Him to Do

The second step we must take on our healing journey is to ask God for our miracle. I love how the New Living Translation begins this leper's story with the word "suddenly." One day you are fine, and the next, you are not. One day you are well, and then "suddenly" you need a miracle.

So, *suddenly*, this man approached Jesus and asked if Jesus was willing to heal him. I don't know if Jesus is willing to heal you. But I know that He wants you to ask! The Bible teaches us that we do not receive answers to prayers that we do not pray. We have not because we ask not (James 4:2). So ask God for what you want. After all,

> You will never know God's will for your miracle unless you ask for the miraculous.

what do you have to lose if you really need a miracle?

That's exactly what my young pastor friend and his wife did. They asked God for a miracle. They cried out to God and anointed his wife's belly with oil, begging God to have mercy and heal their son. You will never know God's will for your miracle unless you ask for the miraculous.

Maintain a Posture of Reverence

The third step on your journey to discover God's will is to maintain a posture of reverence. Notice that the man knelt before the Lord. If you're in need of a miracle, I know you are suffering. But we are in no place to demand anything from God. It's okay to pray with passion like Natasha did in chapter 5. It's okay to find your voice. It is never okay to be disrespectful. God doesn't owe anyone anything. He has already given you and me eternal life if we've asked. He does not have to provide us with everything we want. Even Jesus, before He went to the cross for you and me, knelt before the Lord as He prayed.

If Jesus knelt when He prayed, then you and I should kneel. We must adopt a posture of humility when we ask for the miraculous. I remind myself this way: *whenever I seek God's presence, I must have a posture of reverence.*

The book of Hebrews explicitly addresses how Jesus prayed with reverence:

> While Jesus was here on earth, he offered prayers and pleadings, with a loud cry and tears, to the one who could rescue him from death. And God heard his prayers because of his deep reverence for God. (5:7 NLT)

Reverence is something that has gotten lost in our culture. It's okay to be casual with many things; just don't be casual with God when you need something. If you mean to pray like your life or someone else's life depends on God's miraculous power, then let that be reflected in your posture and attitude. Notice that Hebrews 5:7 says that God heard Jesus' prayers because of His deep reverence. Show God you are serious. Don't be afraid to bow your head or close your eyes when you pray. Don't be afraid to fall on your knees.

In church, I am always amazed that when I say, "Every head bowed and every eye closed," there are always a few people in every service looking right back at me. We bow our heads when we pray in church out of reverence. We close our eyes to help us focus our minds on what we are praying. Always adopt a posture of humility. It's not meant to make you feel weird but to help you feel God when you need Him most. Although Jesus did not get a yes to His request when He prayed and showed reverence before God, He did get a yes to the presence of God. So humble yourself when you pray, especially for a miracle.

When we pray for a miracle, we believe that God can, and then we ask that He will, and then we wait for His answer.

Ultimately, true reverence is about releasing. This is the hardest part of reverence. Reverence says, "I'm not God; You are. I will accept whatever You decide." Jesus modeled this specifically in the garden of Gethsemane when He prayed, "Father, if you are willing, please take this cup of suffering away from me. Yet I want your will to be done, not mine" (Luke 22:42 NLT).

Jesus asked for a miracle but ultimately released His answer to the wisdom of God. We aren't the ones with the power when it comes to the miracles we receive. So ask for your miracle passionately, but be ready to accept whatever answer God gives you. To pray for God's will is to be willing to accept God's answer even if, like Jesus before the cross, it's not what you want.

This is exactly what we see the leprous man do. He said, "Lord, if you are willing, you can make me clean" (Matthew 8:2 NIV). We ask for what we *want* and then *wait* for the answer that will reveal God. Remind yourself as you wait for God's answer that every prayer is answered with yes, no, or wait. But all prayers are answered, so listen for the voice of Jesus.

Listen for the Voice of Jesus

As you seek God's will for your miracle, the fourth step is to listen for His voice. The leprous man asked, knelt, and waited for Jesus to answer. Jesus said some of the most beautiful words ever recorded—*I am willing*.

Jesus reached out and touched him. "I am willing," he said. "Be healed!" And instantly the leprosy disappeared. (Matthew 8:3 NLT)

It's not just the man who cried out to Jesus who heard, "I am willing." Many people, including myself, have heard these exact words right before we were healed. Remember Mitch, from chapter 6, who had to wait for three years to be healed from his crippling disease? In the moment before he was healed, he heard the voice of God say, *I am willing.* And then he was healed.

The words and the healing do not always happen as closely as they did for Mitch and the man with leprosy in Matthew 8.

As I mentioned, my back was out when I was meant to be writing the chapter on waiting for healing. I was laid out on the floor for almost two weeks, unable to finish. As I cried out to God, "Please heal me!" I heard repeatedly, *I am willing. I am willing.* Fortunately, I was healed without surgery. I needed to be touched by someone with the gift of healing.

We can all pray for healing, and God can channel His power through any of us. But there are some people within the church whom God uses more than others to bring about healing. The Bible calls them people with the gift of healing (1 Corinthians 12:9). I know two people whom God consistently uses to bring about miraculous healing. God does not always heal through them, but He heals through them way more often than what I've seen done through others.

The first healer I know is an actual doctor. He is schooled in medicine, but his faith runs deep in the Lord. I have seen him heal with modern Western medicine, and I have repeatedly seen him heal with prayer. He is so good at it, I introduce him as a healer. What I love about him is that he can heal the body, heart, and soul.

The second is my wife. When she prays, God answers. So much so that sometimes I feel like I need to remind God who the pastor is! I have seen her pray for the impossible, and then I have watched in absolute amazement as it happened right in front of me.

The most recent case was when she prayed for a woman named Kathie, who was diagnosed with terminal ovarian cancer. My wife prayed over her and cried out to God for miraculous healing. The woman went in for surgery and had a complete hysterectomy. The surgery was a success, but the hospital panicked. They found *no* signs of cancer anywhere in anything they removed. The hospital was so shocked, they were worried about a lawsuit, but the woman and my wife knew it was a miracle. Jesus said, "I am willing," and then He touched her.

Don't be afraid to ask for people to pray over you. Jesus can borrow the hands of His people to heal your disease. Often, He does it through people with the spiritual gift of healing, but He can do it through anyone with the faith to believe. God used both my doctor and my wife to bring about my healing. God was willing to heal me. I heard that every time I prayed. But His will was not to heal me until I asked my wife and doctor to pray over me. Only then was I dramatically healed.

Mitch's own miracle came after a bunch of college kids anointed him with oil and prayed, and then he was healed. They simply cried out to God, "We know You can; we pray that You will." Then Mitch's friends placed their hands on him and asked for a miracle. They got one, and Mitch's life was changed. Don't be afraid to let God borrow your hands or someone else's hands to perform one of His miracles.

Surrender to Whatever God Has for You

The next step on the road map to discovering God's will is huge. As you listen for the voice of Jesus, He may ask you to do something to experience your miraculous healing.

Jesus didn't just heal the man with leprosy; He gave him a mission. Jesus told the man He had healed, "Don't tell anyone about this. Instead, go to the priest and let him examine you. Take along the offering required in the law of Moses for those who have been healed of leprosy. This will be a public testimony that you have been cleansed" (Matthew 8:4 NLT).

Can you imagine receiving such a miracle and Jesus instructing you to tell no one? If I had received that kind of miracle, I would have wanted to tell everyone immediately. But Jesus had a different plan. Jesus also told the man to go to the priest and to make an offering. Understand this: you cannot buy a miracle. Jesus had more in mind than a mere offering. Jesus wanted to make a powerful point. Often, as we seek His will, His plan differs significantly from ours. As you seek God's will, you also have a mission. That mission is to remain obedient no matter how difficult or strange obedience appears.

You may be tempted to go rogue when you need a miracle for whatever reason. You may consider compromising your morals and your Christian values. Don't! We may not know what God's will is for your miracle, but we know what God's will is for your morality. Don't compromise. The second you compromise to the will of others, you are out of the will of God that you seek.

My young pastor friend and his wife were given medical permission to terminate their son's life. He told me that they weren't sure of much, but they knew that no matter what, termination was not what God wanted them to do. They both made the difficult but right choice to give their son and God's miraculous power a chance.

Their son was born, and a part of his brain is still missing. But nothing is missing from his personality. They watch him closely. It's been several years now, and their son is loving, smart, and can walk and talk. He will be in school soon. He is a miracle!

As you process God's will for your miracle, the last step is to ask if there is something God wants you to do and then surrender to whatever it is. Our attention is almost always focused on the here and now. God is focused on forever. As you seek God's will for your miracle, consider that God may use the storm to give you a new assignment.

When I first met Ryan, I didn't know his name. I called him "Oxygen Guy" because he was walking with an oxygen tank when I saw him in our church lobby. I was preaching through a series on healing. I wrongly assumed that he wanted prayer for healing or some miracle. So as he approached, I asked him, "Do you need a prayer for a miracle?"

Ryan shocked me when he said, "No, I am a miracle."

Ryan was twenty-nine and in the navy. He was a SERE instructor, which stands for Survival, Evasion, Resistance, and

Escape. His job was to train and prepare those in the military most at risk for capture. Ryan had been strong, young, and healthy. Then he wasn't. The day after Christmas, Ryan's life changed forever when he got COVID. Many people who got COVID had mild symptoms. Ryan's were severe, and he almost died.

Ryan was so sick that he was transferred to three different hospitals over a couple of months and his story made the local news. His beloved wife pleaded openly for the community to pray, and she came forward at our church to pray for a miracle. As Ryan's condition worsened, the naval hospital called her to come and say goodbye. He was coding, and it didn't look good.

Right before Ryan went into a coma, he cried out to God. He knew his condition was grave and that if he went into a coma, there was a strong chance he would not come out. Separated from the world by tubes, glass, and machines monitoring his every breath, he prayed directly from his heart to God's. As a young man, Ryan had always been told by his believing father that there was a call on his life, and Ryan knew that call was to serve God at church. But Ryan had fallen in love with his career and fallen away from his calling. Now Ryan prayed, "God, if You get me out of this and heal me, I will do whatever You want me to do." He didn't know how he would serve, but he knew that if he were healed, serving God was exactly what he would do.

Ryan's last memory before the coma was of his wife, outside the room on the other side of the glass, with tears in her eyes. Before he closed his eyes, he read her lips as she said, "It's gonna be okay."

Ryan went into a medically induced sleep. His lungs were so bad he had his blood transferred out of his body into a machine. The machine put the oxygen he desperately needed into his blood and circulated it back into his body. Even though Ryan's condition was grave, his wife, family, and church relied on God's grace. Even though Ryan was disconnected from the world by a coma, he was not disconnected from God. While Ryan slept, his deceased father appeared to him, speaking vividly.

He later recalled that his father was stern but clear when he said, "You made promises to Jesus when you were younger. Are you ready to fulfill your promise?" Jesus was willing to heal Ryan if he was ready to serve Him.

Ryan responded, "Yes, I am ready." In the vision, his father reached out and touched him, and then immediately Ryan woke up. He had been in a coma for weeks and had lost track of his life for months. He went into the hospital at an incredibly fit 190 pounds and came out weighing less than 140. He was awakened at one of the nation's leading hospitals and led by God into a different mission.

I met Ryan, the "Oxygen Guy," just three days after he was released from the hospital. His voice was still hoarse. "I am ready to serve," he told me. He had been healed by God, not to return to the way things were but to embrace a new mission to tell the world how things can be.

Today, Ryan is alive and healthy. His lungs would not allow him to continue his career in the military. Still, his miracle would allow him to continue in his calling. What I love about Ryan is that he has remained faithful to his release to God's will. He has surrendered his life to whatever

God wants. He is healthy and happy to serve wherever God has him. And he's eager to share his miraculous story of God's healing power.

That's exactly what Jesus did for the man healed of leprosy. He gave him a new mission. All healing miracles are simply an extension of life and a new mission for life! Ryan, too, received an extension. Not to fulfill his old mission of training those captured in battle but a new mission to tell people who have been captured by sin about Jesus.

> **All healing miracles are simply an extension of life and a new mission for life!**

Jesus sent the leper not to his family but to Jerusalem. He sent the man whose life had been saved to the city that would soon take His life. Jesus wanted the priests in Jerusalem to publicly confirm His miraculous healing power. The purpose of the offering was simply to show that Jesus was not against Jewish law, in order to open the hearts of some of the priests serving in Jerusalem to recognize that He came to fulfill God's law. After all, Jesus was not against God; He was and is God's only Son, who came to heal and save the sick (Luke 19:10).

So as you pray for God's will for your miracle, remember to

- trust in what God can do;
- ask God for what you want Him to do;
- maintain a posture of reverence;
- listen for the voice of Jesus; and
- surrender to whatever God has for you.

As you seek God's will for your miracle, know that God is seeking you. No matter the outcome, you are loved and matter deeply to God. You and I don't always get what we want. That's the harsh reality of asking God for a supernatural work. But there is good news. God always gets what He wants for those who are in Christ.

He gets you.

I don't know if you will get your miracle now. Still, because of Jesus, you will get countless miracles forever in eternity with Jesus.

PRAY

Lord Jesus, help me to trust in Your power. This thing I am facing is too big for me, but I know it is nothing for You. I ask specifically that You answer my prayer with a yes. God, I know I am in no position to demand anything. Thank You for everything You have already given me. I await Your answer. I pray that You are willing, but ultimately, I surrender to whatever Your will is.

WATCH

REFLECT

1. Why do you think it is so hard to know God's will when it comes to miracles?
2. Have you ever experienced someone who claimed to know God's will, but it didn't happen? What can you learn from that experience?
3. How can focusing on God's power help you with confidence as you pray for miracles?
4. Where do you need to grow in reverence as you pray? And what must you do to position yourself to better hear God's voice?
5. How can you grow in trusting God when it comes to things you don't understand?

NINE

THE COMPLEX REALITY OF HEALING

THANK YOU FOR MAKING ME SO WONDERFULLY COMPLEX!

YOUR WORKMANSHIP IS MARVELOUS—HOW WELL I KNOW IT.
PSALM 139:14 NLT

Miracles happen every day, but not for everyone. If they did, we wouldn't call them miracles; we would call them normal. Even with all our medical and scientific advances, it's still called a medical *practice* because healing is complicated, even for those with all kinds of medical expertise and training.

There is nothing simple about healing a person because there is nothing simple about you. The Bible teaches that God made you "wonderfully complex" (Psalm 139:14 NLT). This complexity is wonderful when things are working but incredibly frustrating and difficult to understand when they are not. I believe it is our assumptions that often get in the way of the healing miracle we seek.

When people come to church for healing, they often assume that prayer is all they need. As people of faith, we tend to see all problems as spiritual in nature. As Christians, we fail to realize that something deeper may be going on that requires more than prayer for healing. Our problem may require medical attention. We may even need medication to experience relief from our suffering.

Western medicine is often the exact opposite. They assume you are merely a biological machine. If they can give you a tune-up or make a change to your chemistry, you will be well. Sometimes Western medicine does not make people *well* but actually makes people *worse*. In the church, many people snub their noses at science and Western medicine. There is a deep sense of mistrust when it comes to the medical and scientific community. Some of that mistrust is warranted, and some is not. These people believe that all they need is God, and they often suffer and, in some cases, die for their ignorance.

My friends in the science community are the opposite. They fail to see the need for spiritual care. They view the spiritual side of people as make-believe. Their education has made them arrogant. When a patient does not respond to their medicine, they tend not to look deeper. They refuse to ask more questions and simply dismiss the patient as the unlucky percentage, those who do not respond to treatment.

Sometimes a person cannot find healing in either Western medicine or in the church through prayer. Sometimes they need the pastor and the doctor to work together because the problem is more complex than either field alone can understand. If we close the gap between the scientific and faith communities, we can help more people who are suffering, especially those who suffer from mental illness.

AN EXAMPLE OF COMPLEX HEALING

Over my years of pastoring, I have seen many people battle diseases. I have seen God do truly miraculous things, and I have watched people suffer horrific levels of pain with no relief. I always rejoice at the miracles and struggle through the suffering of others, especially when it involves children. One of the most frustrating cases I have ever experienced involved a young girl in our church who was adopted. For her protection, I will use the name Lily.

Lily suffered abuse and neglect during the first four years of her life. The frequent abuse, multiple moves, and uncertainty of where she would be from day to day took its toll on this precious girl until she spun completely out of control. Everything was hard for her. It was also extremely hard on those who loved her and tried to help her. Like so many kids today, Lily's life was messed with before she was ever born. Not by God or because of God but because of the brokenness of people and humanity's addiction to sin.

Her mother was a teenager who was involved in drugs and gangs. She was hooked on drugs as Lily grew in her womb. Lily's introduction to life on earth was absolute chaos. Her earliest memories were of hunger, trauma, abandonment, and fear. At the age of two, her guardian became the State of California. When she went into the system, she had few teeth because they had all rotted out from being left daily in a crib with a bottle of milk and little else.

Lily's struggle was not over once she was taken from her birth family; California's foster care system is far from what it should be. She moved between seven different foster care homes in two years. Some of the care she received as a ward of the state was worse than the neglect she had endured from her biological mother. At age four and a half, she was adopted by a family in our church. They had lost multiple children to miscarriages and were full of hope and joy to have a child to love and care for. For a time, things were okay.

One summer evening when Lily was nine years old, her adoptive dad was unexpectedly called to work for an emergency. It was late at night, and his leaving home so abruptly was not something Lily was used to. She asked her adoptive mom where he was going, and she was told that there was an emergency he had to take care of. In a panic, Lily asked if her dad was coming home or if he was leaving them for good. Her mom held her close and assured her that he would be back. Because of Lily's life experience up to that point, she had no reason to believe that this was not like every other time, and in her mind, she prepared for the worst.

Something changed that night in Lily. Watching her father leave unexpectedly triggered the pain, fear, and abandonment she was so used to. She snapped. Almost overnight, Lily became erratic and uncontrollable. It was as if her mind had been hijacked and her body was just a prisoner along for the ride.

Lily began having extreme fits of rage and bouts of violence. Her strength in those moments was something more like that of an adult. Her father struggled to restrain her (for her safety) when she was out of control. She punched and kicked holes in the walls and would throw and break anything she could get her hands on—even things bolted to the walls. She screamed for what seemed like hours on end, physically attacked her family, and ended her rages in what was best described as a trance—repeating the same words as she rocked back and forth. Her family sought help from psychologists, psychiatrists, therapists, and all the resources they could find. Lily was placed on a slew of antipsychotic medicines with the prayer that each med would be the one that helped ease her pain.

Eventually, Lily's behavior became so violent that the police had to be involved. Her adoptive parents were devastated. Their little girl was broken and terrifying to be around. Lily was put on a seventy-two-hour psychiatric hold and hospitalized for her safety and the safety of others. She was officially diagnosed with a laundry list of psychological disorders. The doctors did all they could to treat each problem, but every medicine they tried only made things worse—and many created new problems. Her past trauma had been awakened and wreaked havoc on her soul.

The doctors recommended that Lily be moved, for a time, to full-time residential care and supervision at a children's psychiatric center. Even away at a full-time facility, Lily struggled. She routinely got into physical altercations with the other children in the program. She regularly eloped (a clinical term for running away) and, at one point, climbed onto the roof, running back and forth on the sloped tiles, screaming. She broke most of the rules and even ripped the braces off her teeth one bracket at a time with pliers she had stolen. She was on a path to becoming a full-time ward of the state.

No one could understand why, even with our prayers, she was getting worse. Lily was getting the best medical care money could buy. She had love and support from home and a church family crying out to God for healing. Nothing seemed to help. She continued to get worse, and her parents were losing hope. We were losing Lily.

If someone you love is battling mental illness, it can be terrifying. You can begin by being worried about your loved one and end up worrying about your own safety. I regularly talk with people who don't know what to do or whom to turn to when someone they love is battling a mental illness like Lily was. I tell them the same thing I am writing here. *We turn to Jesus.* He is our rock and is not afraid to deal with those battling mental health issues.

A ROAD MAP FOR THOSE BATTLING MENTAL ILLNESS

Each of the four Gospels details Jesus' encounters with, and healings of, those with mental illness. A specific story in Mark 5 serves as a road map for those with mental health concerns. From this story, we learn five things we can do to bring healing to those whose minds are not as they should be.

Deal with the Problem

We first learn from Jesus that we must *deal with it*. Jesus never shied away from those who were struggling mentally. For far too long, Christians have pretended that mental health was not an issue among our ranks—when it always has been. Mental illness does not go away. It does not get better with time. In my experience, it usually gets worse if we ignore it or pretend it does not exist.

In Mark 5, Jesus headed across the Sea of Galilee to a strange land to deal with a strange man. He did this to point the way. When Jesus arrived on the shores of the Gerasenes, He was confronted by a man with mental health issues. The man was out of his mind and not wearing clothes.

Recently, my wife sent me on an errand to develop some film. I asked who develops film these days, and she said, "We do!" So I went. Something caught my attention as I stood in line at a local Walgreens. A woman standing behind me was missing her pants! California is overrun with people who are losing their battle with mental illness. Society has turned its back on them, and in many cases, they have turned to self-medicating with drugs and alcohol.

I turned around to ask if I could help her. She did not respond but only stared; it was as if she was staring straight through me. She was clothed only in an ill-fitting, filthy T-shirt full of holes. She had no shoes, underwear, or sense of her present reality or condition. Her body twitched uncontrollably as she turned away from me and stumbled down the liquor aisle. She grabbed two twelve-packs of beer and walked out of the store. She was not stopped for stealing—or for being partially naked.

Our society has made little progress in the last two thousand years in supporting and treating people with severe mental illness. We often leave them to the streets to cry out for help. However, Jesus hears the cries of the mentally ill, and He does not try to avoid them but goes all in to reach them! If this is your current battle, go all in! Jesus will meet you no matter where you are. In Mark 5, He proved this by going to where this man was.

Eliminate the Stigma of Mental Illness

The second thing we need to see is that Jesus removed the shame of mental illness. No one picks their disease; it picks us. You should not be ashamed of a broken mind any more than you should be ashamed of a broken leg! Life happens, and things break. There is nothing to be ashamed of.

One of my spiritual mentors was Pastor Glen. He was a giant in the faith. He was both a pastor and a counselor to me. In my last conversation with him before he died, he said, "Matt, I got the dementia!" Then he laughed and said, "Well, at least that's what they tell me." Glen was an example to me to the very end. He was a mentor in health and in sickness. He wasn't ashamed of his illness. He was just honest. Jesus said, "The truth will set you free" (John 8:32). Being honest about your struggle is a big part of your victory! If you or someone you love isn't in their right mind, own it. The truth is always healing.

The subtitle for Mark 5 in the Bible, no matter the translation, will say something like, "Jesus Heals a Demon-Possessed Man." But that's not how the text describes him. The text does not use the language of being mentally ill or demon possessed when the man is first introduced but calls the person "a man with an unclean spirit" (v. 2). As modern readers, we tend to miss this subtle detail. To a first-century Jew, the entire region of the Gerasenes was unclean. The witnesses of this miracle were pig farmers, who, according to Old Testament Jewish law, were the epitome of unclean.

This is a super important step in dealing with mental illness. We must remove the stigma of mental illness. So many people suffer with their thoughts because, as Christians, we have not made room for their illness in our hearts.

Either you or someone you love will struggle with mental illness in your lifetime. Bring this matter to God. God cares so much about mental illness that He made this entire journey to reach this man! Jesus went after this one sheep, even if that sheep was not in his right mind.

Be Real About the Threat of Mental Illness

The third thing we need to realize about severe mental health conditions is that they can be *scary* to deal with. There is no way around this. We need to eliminate the stigma of mental illness but be real about its threat.

As soon as Jesus stepped off the boat, He was confronted with the scary reality of how bad mental illness can be. It's okay to be afraid. The Bible gives a lengthy description of this man. He was so strong he could not be bound by anyone or anything. He was in so much mental anguish he would cut himself with stones. Night and day, he lived among the tombs, crying out. This man was scary.

You can be afraid of mental illness, but know that Jesus is not! The man ran at Jesus, but Jesus did not run. He stood His ground and said, "What is your name?" (v. 9).

Understand There Could Be Multiple Issues

The fourth thing I want you to notice is that before Jesus did a miracle, He wanted to know what He was dealing with, and the answer is profound. The man said,

My name is Legion, for we are many. (v. 9)

This is so important for all of us seeking the miracle that seems to evade us. The man's problem had a name, and its name was "many." So as Christians, we say he had many demons, and medical professionals would say he had multiple psychological disorders. I think the text means that he had *many* issues. Some were spiritual, some were psychological, and some were relational.

So when you are praying through something and not experiencing the miracle you want, ask yourself if you could be experiencing a "legion" of problems. Too many people today self-diagnose and pray for God to heal a problem they don't have. If Jesus wanted clarity about exactly what He was dealing with, so should we.

Know That Jesus Can Heal Anyone Brought to Him

After Jesus diagnosed the problem, He sent "Legion" away into a great herd of pigs, and the man was completely changed (vv. 11–15). The pigs Jesus sent them into drowned themselves in the lake because that's what the devil does. He destroys whatever he inhabits. He is the opposite of Jesus, who saves whoever invites Him in. This is the last thing I want you to notice: Jesus can heal anyone who is brought to Him!

THREE WAYS DEMONS CAN AFFECT US

As I have pored over this story in Mark 5 repeatedly, I noticed three ways this demon affected this man.

Spiritually

First, this man's problem, which affected him physically and mentally, was a spiritual problem. We must understand that spiritual problems cannot be solved through traditional medical means. A demon will not respond positively to Xanax.

Jesus immediately recognized that the devil was involved in this man's issues. For far too long, our psychological community has ignored the role that the spiritual world plays in mental health.

As you reread the story in Mark 5, it's hard to tell when the man is speaking and when the demon is speaking. We don't know precisely when something is purely mental and when something is spiritual. I think that's why Jesus asked his name, because whenever the devil is present, so is confusion.

Psychologically

After Jesus miraculously removed the demon from the man, the healing was not over. The formerly possessed and naked man was now fully clothed and in his right mind! The local pig farmers were so frightened by this exorcism that they fled back to town. When they came back, they saw the man sitting and talking with Jesus.

This is an important step to healing. Jesus didn't just cast out the demon; He sat with the man and counseled him. Jesus didn't just get rid of the problem; He gave the man what he needed. When you are looking for your miracle, you may need more than the problem solved. You may need to sit with Jesus.

When the villagers returned, they asked Jesus to leave—and He did. Jesus never forces Himself on anyone. The man who was formerly possessed begged to go with Jesus. But Jesus refused. This is hard to understand, but it was vital for this man's complete healing. The man had lived alone for years—all alone with his pain and his torment. His only companions were the dead people below him in the graveyard he called home. His family and all his friends had given up on him.

Jesus knew this man needed spiritual deliverance, psychological counseling, and relational restoration with those he had been kept apart from. So Jesus sent him back to his community, not as a broken person with a frightening personality but as a healed man with a testimony of God's goodness. Only when this man went home and told others how he was healed would his healing be complete. He could not be completely healed unless all three of these issues—spiritual, psychological, and relational—were dealt with.

This threefold healing was exactly what Lily needed.

Lily lived away from her parents in residential treatment for a little over a year. Then suddenly, the COVID pandemic shut down the world and, along with it, the residential treatment facility where Lily was living. All children with families were sent back home with a prescription and their best wishes. Children who were not sent home would have had to stay on lockdown without being able to see their families for the duration of the pandemic. Lily's parents had missed her and had prayed for the day she would return, but they were terrified about her coming home so abruptly.

Her father rallied several leaders in our church to come and pray. We could not pray over Lily because she would not allow it at the time. So some of the men from our church came and prayed over the house, crying out to God to free Lily from whatever enslaved her. God was gracious, and the Holy Spirit moved. Lily was compliant when she came home but was far from healed.

Remember, Jesus taught us that when it comes to mental health we have to go at it and go all in, and that's exactly what Lily's parents did. Lily didn't just have a spiritual problem. She wasn't in her right mind! She needed a doctor who understood the complex nature of healing regarding mental health. They found one in Dr. Amen. What a name! *Amen* means true, and that's exactly what his team did; they went after the truth.

Dr. Amen is a psychiatrist and brain disorder specialist. His team performed a scan of Lily's brain and found what they believed was the problem. Three parts of her brain were on overdrive, constantly firing, and others were dark and not working at all. From their experience, one *specific* medication targeted those areas—a medicine other doctors had not tried. Her daily meds were reduced from a handful to *just two*. Lily showed almost instant improvement—but she was still not totally healed.

Many of my Christian friends frown upon taking medication for mental illness. They see it as a lack of faith or a lack of strength. But if you need medication and don't take it, I think it reveals a lack of wisdom. Some of us need eyeglasses to help us see, and some don't. You don't have a lack of faith if you wear eyeglasses. For some people, our brains *need* medication, not to help us see but to help us think more clearly, and in turn they help us better see and deal with our thoughts and emotions. I have seen medication help many faithful people who trust God. If you or a family member needs medication, you should not feel ashamed but thrilled that it is available.

I have been in a small group for years with a dear friend.

He loves Jesus but battles the thoughts in his mind and the emotions those thoughts create. Week after week, we would talk in small group about his depression and anxiety. We read Scripture and prayed for healing, but my friend did not get better. He got horribly worse. He believed that his faith in God and knowledge of Scripture were enough to heal him. But his mental illness was swallowing his personality, and we were losing him.

I am not saying that God can't heal without medication. God can do whatever He wants. Jesus did not need medicine to heal the possessed man in Mark 5. But you and I are not Jesus; sometimes we need medical help as we pursue our miracle.

My friend almost lost everything before we finally held an intervention. Our entire small group met and asked him to see a psychiatrist. Our intervention hurt his feelings but ultimately led to him being set free from his crippling thoughts. The medication helped restore his personality. He went from a depressed young man with no energy and no desire to live to a vibrant, loving member of our small group who even got married to a wonderful woman. It wasn't his *faith* that was off; it was his *chemistry*, and a pill changed that!

Medication will help, but *alone* it will not heal. Think of medication for your brain like a steroid for your body. Your body only gets buff if you take steroids *and* work out. I am not encouraging you to take steroids! Just trying to make a point. I have seen too many people taking medication while not working out their brains in counseling. The man in Mark 5 needed to talk with Jesus even after his mind was set free. You may need to talk with a medical professional or therapist who knows Jesus and understands mental illness. You must be willing to do whatever it takes to address your wound.

Relationally

Lily, too, had wounds that weren't just spiritual and psychological; they were also relational. As a young child, she did not receive little hugs—only *big* wounds. She learned that those closest to her were the greatest threat to her. In her mind, love was dangerous, and family was never safe. She wasn't ready to trust others just yet. This wasn't her fault. As a victim of abuse, it was just her experience.

Lily's adoptive family found a therapist who got Lily working with animals. Some animals are scary, but most are not nearly as scary as people. Animals are always exactly who they are; people can pretend to be what they are not. Slowly but surely, Lily learned it was okay to care, and then she learned it was okay to love. Animals taught her how to feel. They taught her that she was needed. In caring for animals, Lily learned that things could heal. By helping animals, she began to heal.

I recently went out to dinner with Lily and her family. This is something that would have been impossible at one time. I don't think we could have gotten through a meal at their house, much less out in public. During the entire meal, I couldn't stop looking at Lily. She sat next to me, completely in her right mind.

I believe in miracles because I have seen them, and at dinner that night, *a miracle was sitting next to me.*

Lily is now a teenager, a beautiful young woman. She attends a regular school. She sits in a class and relates to students and has incredible friends. I recently ran into her after a church service. She waited in line without her parents to talk with me. The line was long, but she waited as patiently as a saint. I gave her a hug and asked her how she was doing. She said she was great, but her eyes said something else. I asked, "Are you okay?" and she said yes. She said, "Your sermon spoke to my heart," and she said she liked it. She told me she hears God when I speak and always gets so much out of the messages. I said, "Lily, you have changed." She said, "I have, Pastor Matt." She said she had given her life to Jesus.

Lily went from a scary girl screaming into the air and at anyone who tried to help her, to a girl who was aware of her identity as a child of God and could *hear* Jesus, even from a sinner like me! Jesus can do this if we press in and don't give up! If we eliminate the shame and stigma behind mental illness and go all in, the same way as Jesus did, we can see miracles. We can see people delivered who are trapped in their minds. We can see Jesus heal people like Lily. Today she is in her right mind, has a new heart and, because of Jesus, a new life. She even has a new name. That was her doing. She wanted a new name for her new life.

We can have so much more deliverance if, like in the case of Lily, we follow the healing path of Jesus. Mental illness is a complex issue. We don't always know what part of the struggle is mental, spiritual, or relational, but if we go all in and treat all three areas, the way Jesus did, I think we will help and heal many more people.

PRAY

Lord Jesus, give me the strength to do whatever it takes to be in my right mind. Help me to explore the broken areas of my life and to seek healing. I invite the Holy Spirit to direct me to whatever healing I might need—whether it is spiritual, psychological, or relational. I pray this in Your name, amen.

WATCH

REFLECT

1. How have you personally experienced the complex nature of healing?
2. How can you as a Christian integrate spiritual, psychological, and relational healing into understanding how God might heal?
3. How can you work to narrow the gap between medical and spiritual communities regarding healing?
4. How can you eliminate the shame and stigma of mental health in your church community?
5. Who are some people battling mental health issues you can pray for and work to help heal?

TEN

THE POWER OF SPIRITUAL HEALING

"SIMON, SIMON, SATAN HAS
ASKED TO SIFT EACH OF YOU
LIKE WHEAT."

LUKE 22:31 NLT

S piritual healing does not come from within or without
but comes only from above and through the power of
Jesus. You and I are engaged in a spiritual war, and that war
has physical casualties. These casualties often occur in the
lives of those who look the most perfect.

When I first met Emma, her life seemed perfect. She
was beautiful, talented, and successful. Like many women

with her looks and talent, she was trying to make it as an actress and performer in Hollywood. It seemed as if there wasn't anything she couldn't do. Her career was growing. She had the smile of a Disney princess and the integrity of a saint. When my kids were little, she would make it a point to say hello or give them a wink as she performed! Acting and performing seemed effortless for her.

One of the things I loved about her was that attention did not seem to change her. I could watch her on TV on Saturday night and would see her in church on Sunday. She was serious about her career, and she was serious about Jesus.

Emma was all in for the silver screen until she fell in love with her husband. They were the perfect couple. Barbie had found her Ken. Soon after they were married, she lost her love for Hollywood and found a love for family. She walked away from fame without even the slightest regret. But there was something that would not let her go.

Emma, her husband, and I had developed a relationship through premarital counseling, and I was blessed to perform their wedding. They rode off into the sunset to their happily ever after, just like in the performances I had watched her in. But things did not go happily for very long.

Soon after they got married, Emma began to have horrible nightmares. They went from dreams at night to physical encounters even after she was awake. While sleeping, she awakened to something unseen smothering and pushing her with force into the mattress. Her husband was frightened and wanted to help, but he did not know what to do. One night, it was so bad that she felt hot hands pressing against her body. When she woke, she had red marks all over her body where *something* had pushed her and held her down. She panicked and couldn't recover. Her husband scooped her up and headed to the emergency room. She was in total panic and struggled to breathe.

At the hospital, Emma and her husband waited helplessly in the waiting room. She thought she was going crazy. Once she was finally seen and showed the doctor the red marks left all over her body, the doctor told her she was having a panic attack. They gave her Benadryl and sent her home. Even with the antihistamine, she could not go back to sleep. Emma had been up all night with no relief. That morning was a Sunday, so she called her parents and asked them to meet her at Sandals Church.

I met her outside on our church patio between services as I greeted people. She looked tired, and her hair was not combed. I could tell she was not okay. I had met her parents at the wedding, and I knew something had happened by the look of them all. All four of them—Emma, her mom and dad, and her husband—walked straight toward me. Emma asked if we could talk somewhere in private. We headed to a counseling office, and everyone was silent when the door closed behind us. I had no idea what I was in for.

She blurted out, "Pastor Matt, something's wrong with me." She told me about the nightmares and feeling pressed into her mattress. She told me she thought what was happening was real but was worried she was going crazy. Her husband mouthed the words "Help us," not wanting to rattle Emma any more than she already was.

I said to her, "How can I help?" She began to remove her shirt. I looked at her parents, who were unfazed by this action. Her father looked me dead in the eye and motioned for me to look. I was uncomfortable and had no idea what she would show me. She removed her shirt and said, "I am not crazy. Look." Her torso was covered in bright-red handprints, not like bruises but more like mild burns. The hospital had diagnosed her with some sort of allergic reaction. The handprints were on her stomach, chest, and back, and one was wrapped around her neck. They were clearly handprints. How on earth the hospital did not come to the same conclusion is beyond me.

I looked at her husband, and knowing what I was about to ask, he quickly said, "Those are not my handprints," and stepped back.

"What do we do?" Emma asked. I told them we were going to call on the name of Jesus and ask Him to take away whatever this was.

She had left Hollywood, but something had come with her that did not like that she was gone. We asked Jesus to take *it* away, and *He* did. It's been years since that Sunday afternoon. Since then, she has had no demonic dreams and no handprints, no returns to the emergency room—nothing, just the blessing of lots of babies and the peace of mind that only Jesus can give.

Emma's case was easy; the hospital had been confused, but our faith in Jesus clarified the problem. Cases involving spiritual warfare are not always so easily detected. That's because the devil can never *invade* your life; he can only *attach* to something in it.

I grew up in a Baptist church. I'm sure the devil was

everywhere, but we didn't see him or talk about him being anywhere. Most churches fall into one of two camps: it is always the devil's fault, or it's never his fault. I grew up thinking everything was my fault. In my story, the Enemy attached himself to my guilt.

I have always been an achiever. I strive to do the best I can. To me, the only thing worse than death is failure. I would rather die than fail, which is interesting because I have not yet died but have failed more times than I can count. As an achiever, I have sought every type of recognition. After I became a pastor, I sought academic recognition. I only became good at school once I was called to ministry. Once I found something I cared deeply about, learning became much easier. It didn't matter if the teacher was good or bad, engaging or boring. I wanted to learn about God, so I did. After completing my master's degree, I convinced my wife that I should pursue my doctorate, so I did. I found the classes easy and engaging.

Then something began to change. The church I led was growing, and I was excelling academically, but something was happening to me. Something I had never experienced before. I couldn't put my finger on it, but I thought counseling might help. It didn't. I grew more frustrated and more concerned. I wasn't depressed, but I wasn't right. I started having trouble sleeping and lost my love for exercise. I just wasn't myself.

My body began to ache. My hands hurt, my back was stiff, and I had headaches almost daily. I was miserable. My closest friends could tell something was off but chalked it up to stress or my always faithful friend ADHD. I tried praying and fasting and more counseling. Nothing worked.

One day at church, my wife was helping me reorganize the books in my office. We went through my books one by one. She would ask, "Trash or shelf?" If I said, "Trash," that's where it went. If I replied, "Shelf," she would organize it by category, color, and alphabet. My wife is amazing at organization—I am not.

She came to a book I had forgotten about. In my doctoral program, we were given assigned reading and recommended reading. The assigned reading was a ton, so I read very little of the recommended stuff. She held up a book entitled *Defeating Dark Angels* by Dr. Charles Kraft. It had been on the recommended list, so I'd bought it but never really thought about reading it. I laughed out loud and told her I wouldn't read it because I hated the cover design. Remember the old saying "Don't judge a book by its cover"? Well, I had, and I'd been wrong. Tammy held it and said, "Trash or shelf?" I said, "Neither." Something in me felt like I was supposed to read it. So I said, "Backpack!" She looked at me confused, so I again said, "Backpack." She handed it to me, and I put it in my backpack.

Later that night, I did something that changed my life. I read that book.

As I flew through the book's pages, I instantly realized I had been oblivious to what was wrong with me. I wasn't sick, depressed, or stressed. There was nothing wrong with me physically or emotionally. I was under a spiritual attack. I quickly did a Google search, found the author's email, and reached out to him for a one-on-one meeting.

Dr. Kraft did not respond for three months. No matter how much I prayed or confessed, I couldn't shake this feeling of spiritual darkness. I knew my problem but not what it was attached to or how to make it disappear.

Finally, Dr. Kraft responded. He had not ignored my email but had been in Africa. He set a date and time to meet. I don't entirely agree with all of Dr. Kraft's theology. Still, my meeting with him changed my life for the better, and I am eternally grateful. We can all be helped by other Christians, even if there are issues on which we disagree.

I met him at his small office in Pasadena, California. He did not care about his clothes, who I was, or how I was dressed. He was a simple man, a spiritual warrior from a simpler time—the kind that seems hard to find nowadays. He asked how he could help.

I shared with him how I was feeling and what was going on. I asked him if what I was experiencing could be the devil. I will never forget his response. "Oh, you Baptists," he said with a laugh—which I did not think was one bit funny. Then he said, "Of course."

He continued, "The problem is not discovering whether or not this is the devil. The challenge is finding out what the devil has attached himself to in your life."

We started from my childhood and, for two long hours, went well into my thirties. I told him my entire life story, and at the end of the session he told me my problem. He said, "Your problem is guilt. The devil is an accuser and has attached himself to your guilt. You know the gospel; you know Jesus. Now let's preach it to you and not to anyone else."

At that moment, I realized there was some stuff from the past for which I had not allowed myself to be forgiven. I had preached for decades on the power of the blood of Christ. But in my pride, I believed that God's grace was not sufficient for certain sins of mine—because I'd known better when I committed them. That was just the room and leverage the devil needed. I had pushed God's grace out and invited the Enemy's guilt in.

We walked my sin through the reality of what Jesus did for me on the cross. Dr. Kraft asked me which was greater: my sin or Jesus' sacrifice. The answer is evident to anyone who is a Christian. The sacrifice of Jesus was greater. What's so sad is that the guilt I had allowed the devil to hold on to was something I would have told thousands of people in my church to let go of. But *I* didn't. I gave my spiritual enemy a hold on me. I wasn't free. I was in a cage of guilt.

Dr. Kraft reminded me of the grace of the Lord Jesus Christ that I knew was real and free, and that I had already received. He looked at me and then pointed at me. I realized he was pointing through me to something else—to an unwanted guest. He said, "Deception, it's time to go."

I can't fully describe what I felt. It was not something in me but hanging over and behind me, like a super heavy backpack I had been carrying for way too long. It lifted off me, then I felt it go through me as it left. I didn't see it but felt it, and my body physically responded to its exit. I was instantly relieved and felt like I might puke simultaneously. I felt free, and then I felt so dumb.

As a spiritual leader, how was I so blind to my spiritual problem? I walked out of that office determined never to be so fooled by the Enemy again.

In our previous chapter, the man's problem had the name Legion—for he was many (Mark 5:9). That was not the name of my problem. Its name was Deception, and way too many Christians have been fooled by it. Even as faithful believers, we will consider all options when it comes to our healing while ignoring a basic truth about much of the suffering we experience. As Christians, we are often way more scientific than we are spiritual. Not every problem you have is spiritual, but much of your suffering could be.

WHEN SUFFERING IS A SPIRITUAL ATTACK

Jesus tied some physical healing in the Bible to the spiritual oppression we all face. Where you and I see disease, Jesus occasionally saw the devil.

Luke 13 tells us that on one Sabbath, Jesus was teaching in the synagogue. He saw a woman who was entirely bent over as she walked. Every step was a struggle, and she could not stand upright. Her case was severe, and she had suffered from it for years. From our Western perspective, we would assume she had a back injury or was suffering from some sort of disease of the bone or spine.

Jesus saw her, twisted and bent over but trying to get a

glimpse of the Healer as He spoke. She may not have been able to see Him over the crowd, but Jesus could see her. He called her to come closer. Jesus said to the woman, "You are freed from your disability" (v. 12), and He touched her back. She was immediately healed and could stand straight for the first time in years. She was thrilled, but Jesus' critics were not. In the church, we usually focus on their argument about what we can or cannot do on the Sabbath and miss what Jesus identified as the cause of her disease. She had a physical ailment as a result of a spiritual attack (vv. 10–17).

In Jesus' defense of this miracle on the Sabbath, He clearly said that it was not a disease that caused this woman's suffering but the devil himself. He stated that this woman had been bound for eighteen years by Satan. Think about that: for eighteen years this woman, with all of her other responsibilities, had been carrying an unwanted guest on her back. Most Christians will say we cannot be afflicted this way, but notice what Jesus called her. He identified her as "a daughter of Abraham" (v. 16). This means she was on the right side of the spiritual war but was losing this particular battle. Don't ever assume that just because you are a Christian you cannot be attacked or carry evil burdens. The devil can attack what is not his, and he likes to target those who love and serve God.

As a Christian, your soul is safe, but your body is open game for the Enemy's attack. One of the overarching themes of the book of Job is that Satan hates those who love and worship God. It is precisely because Job worshipped God spiritually that Satan attacked him physically. The Bible teaches that all Christians have the Holy Spirit inside them, but some Christians can have the spirit of deception on them!

HOW TO KNOW WHEN PHYSICAL PAIN HAS SPIRITUAL CAUSE

Your illness may not be spiritual, but you are. So don't just pursue physical and emotional well-being but also pursue spiritual health. When I had my deep healing with Dr. Kraft, I was spiritually healed and became physically better. Like the woman who was bound, I was immediately made straight—and you can be too.

So how do you know when your physical pain has a spiritual cause?

A Spirit of Confusion

I have found that the most reliable detector for discovering the presence of the Enemy is a spirit of confusion. If you have been to doctors for physical problems, and they are baffled or express confusion about what's happening to you, that may be a sign that your struggle is not something science can help with.

As a pastor, I have had to face a spirit of confusion many times. One time in particular, I met with a disgruntled member of our church. I took the meeting because I thought he was a sheep God had called me to care for. However, during our time together I discovered that he was a wolf in sheep's clothes.

Have you ever had a fight that got out of control, but halfway through it, you couldn't even remember why you were fighting? That's the Enemy. According to Scripture, our God is "not a God of confusion" (1 Corinthians 14:33). Confusion is *not* the power of the God of heaven but the scheme of the devil.

When I met with this member, there was a coldness. He smiled, but there was no warmth to it. There was something sinister behind the smile—something I could not see but I could sense. He had very unorthodox views regarding the Christian faith, particularly regarding sexuality, and said God had sent him to save our church from our traditional beliefs. In normal circumstances, his views would have been easily dismissed. But this was no normal meeting with an individual; I was meeting with a spirit of confusion. As we talked, I grew confused. I couldn't find my words or make my points. I had my Bible open in front of me. When I wanted to quote scriptures that I had memorized, I couldn't quote it or, to my surprise, even find it in my Bible. It was truly bizarre. I ended the meeting by asking him to leave my office and our church.

I was confused about many things that day, but I knew this man was not a sheep for me to lead but a wolf from which I had to protect my congregation. He met with several staff members before exiting, and when I later asked them how their conversations went, they all answered with similar language: "Confusing, Pastor Matt, strangely confusing."

When you encounter this spirit, please don't argue or engage with it. Don't fall for the Enemy's schemes. Just do what Jesus did: send it away in His name, and get out of there!

A Spirit of Unforgiveness

Scripture teaches us that we are not to be "unaware of [Satan's] schemes" (2 Corinthians 2:11 NIV). Sadly, like I was, this is where many Christians find themselves today.

When the apostle Paul wrote to the Corinthian church, he was writing to help them forgive a fellow member who had sinned against himself and his church community. Even as Christians, it is easy to sin but hard to navigate forgiveness. Many Christians know this verse about not falling for the devil's schemes but are unaware of its context. The context is about how, when, and where to forgive someone. It is precisely in the area of forgiveness that the devil wants to confuse you.

We all struggle with forgiveness because the sins of others have wounded us. A spirit of unforgiveness brings the emotion of anger. It's okay to be angry when someone hurts you. Jesus got angry. It's just not okay to stay that way. Anger is like milk; if you keep it too long, it will go sour. That's why the apostle Paul said, "'In your anger do not sin': Do not let the sun go down while you are still angry, and do not give the devil a foothold" (Ephesians 4:26–27 NIV). Anger is an invitation to the devil to have leverage in our lives.

This leverage pulls us down, and allowing anger to linger can make us

> **Anger is an invitation to the devil to have leverage in our lives.**

sick. No human was meant to carry the spiritual weight of the devil's evil. Christians must remember that this evil can take us down if we are unaware of his schemes.

Prolonged anger is a rejection of the spirit of forgiveness. When I was younger, I was never angry. Early on in my life, nothing bothered me. I could easily let things go. I don't know when or how it happened, but I started hanging on to things. At some point I got angry, stopped forgiving, and Satan began to hang on to me. My inability to forgive myself started because I couldn't forgive others. I am blessed and have never had anything terrible happen to me like I have seen happen to others. I just get hit with a lot of *really* sharp darts. I collect all the darts people throw at me. It's a terrible thing to collect. These darts have hurt me. They don't hurt just when people throw them; they continue to hurt because I keep them.

Prolonged anger is an invitation to the devil and a rejection of God's grace. A rejection of grace is a rejection of the healing power of God. We are not only saved by grace, we are healed by it! When you reject God's healing power, you invite the diseased power of the devil into your life. God's power sets you free. The devil's power weighs you down. If you give the devil enough time, he can break you down—spiritually, emotionally, and even physically.

When I started collecting these darts of people's hurtful words and criticisms, I started giving the devil power in my life. It started with me not forgiving others, and then, because the devil is so good at what he does, I couldn't even forgive myself.

Stop listening to the devil; he loves to whisper in

the ears of believers. Remember, the devil spoke to Jesus (Matthew 4:1–11). Is he speaking to you?

The devil is a master communicator and a master manipulator. If he could convince one-third of heaven's angels to rebel against God, what might he convince you of (Revelation 12:4)?

Usually, the first thing the devil convinces us of is that we don't have to forgive. Forgiveness is not saying that what happened to you is okay. It is saying it's okay to hand this anger over to God. Let Him judge sin, and let your anger go. If you do, the Enemy has to let you go. Remember, he can only hold on to you as long as you hold on to sin.

THE FIRST STEP IN SPIRITUAL HEALING

The first step in spiritual healing is always the truth. It's why Jesus said, "The truth will set you free" (John 8:32)! The devil whispers that you can't be forgiven or you can't forgive someone else, but the cross shouts you can! The devil says you are done, and the resurrected Jesus says you're just getting started. The devil always comes in the form of spiritual deception. It's why Jesus called him a liar (v. 44); you should never trust anything he says. We can trust God's Word to begin spiritual healing and start our journey toward health and wholeness.

James, the half brother of Jesus, also saw a connection between physical illness and sin. He specifically said if any of us as believers are sick, then we should confess our sins to one another so that we can be whole and healed (James 5:14–16). So if you are sick and there is anger, confess it. If there is a lack of forgiveness, give it. Stop listening to the devil; his words only make you sick. The words of Jesus can make you well. Christ makes us well by forgiving us of our sins and helping us forgive the sins of others.

PRAY

Lord Jesus, please forgive me for my sins. Help me forgive myself and those who have sinned against me. Please take away my anger and replace it with Your peace. Take away anything and everything that has given the devil a foothold on my life. Send him away from me, my family, and my home. I pray this in Your name, amen.

WATCH

REFLECT

1. What are some things in your life that may have been a spiritual attack you ignored?
2. What things have you blamed on Satan that you need to take responsibility for?
3. What areas of anger have you not handed over to God that may have handed leverage over to Satan?
4. Which wounds do you need to ask Jesus to heal so you can forgive and move on from the pain Satan can attach to?
5. How can you become more aware of the devil's schemes in your life?

ELEVEN

HEALING EMOTIONAL WOUNDS

THE Lord IS CLOSE TO THE BROKENHEARTED;

HE RESCUES THOSE WHOSE SPIRITS ARE CRUSHED.

PSALM 34:18 NLT

I f we are to pursue healing, we must consider all the ways in which we can hurt. Some wounds are clearly physical, others are spiritual, but often some of our deepest wounds are of the heart. As Christians, we often think we can wave a kind of magic wand, and people will simply be healed and become whole. We don't call it *magic*; we call it an *invitation*. As many churches do, after a service,

Sandals Church invites people to come to the front no matter their need. But some wounds are not healed with just one prayer.

Some can only be healed with a touch from Jesus Himself.

A SLOW JOURNEY OF HEALING

As I've mentioned, when I started our church, I had no idea what I was doing. I only knew one thing: Jesus Christ could change lives. I knew that because He had changed mine. I was naive about how hard it truly is to help heal someone because I was inexperienced with emotional wounding and physical abuse. I'd been raised in a great home. I had two loving parents. They were not perfect, but they were better parents than most of my friends ever dreamed of having. My parents were my protectors; they were never my abusers. I grew up in a home where I knew that there were people I could trust and that there were safe people. I knew my parents would genuinely help me without any desire to hurt me. Many people were not raised in a home like mine. They were not raised with parents who protect but with parents who abuse.

As a young pastor, I wasn't just naive but ambitious. I didn't want to reach other church people; I wanted to reach people no one was reaching, and that's why I was part of a ministry at our church called Jesus Christ's Girls, or JC's Girls for short. No, I wasn't one of the girls. Still, I was the only pastor willing to support this ministry publicly and financially.

JC's Girls was a wild but fantastic idea. We thought we could reach women for Jesus who were still active in the sex industry. The ladies in our church did really unusual things. They went to strip clubs to pray for strippers. They would pay for a lap dance but only ask the dancer if they needed prayer; no one ever received a dance. Ladies from our church would go to porn conventions and offer help to women who wanted to exit the industry. This ministry made way more noise than it ever made a difference. We would have news media both inside and outside our church.

We went viral before that was ever even a thing. Everyone wanted to know about this church in California and this ministry. A Hollywood film director even made a documentary about it called *The Pussycat Preacher*. Like the ministry, it bombed! Soon everyone had an opinion on JC's Girls, and some people stopped calling us Sandals Church and nicknamed us "Scandals Church." The ministry was almost a total failure, not because we didn't try but because we didn't realize how difficult it is to heal the human heart.

The ministry blew up in my face, and close relationships were strained. Some friendships were broken forever. It was so bad I almost wished I never did it. Notice I said I *almost* wished. There was one reason I was glad I was a part of JC's Girls: despite my deadly combination of arrogance and ignorance, God miraculously changed one woman's life through the ministry. I didn't know it then, but she would become a close friend to my wife and me. For this book and at her request, I have changed names in this story.

Mackenzie was one of the hundreds of women I met who found themselves hopelessly trapped in the sex industry. She had never wanted to be a sex worker. It was never a part of her plans. But Mackenzie didn't have parents like mine. Her parents were her abusers. On Mackenzie's twelfth birthday, her mother entered her bedroom and said some men wanted to meet her. Mackenzie had no idea what she was in for that night; how could she? At the age of twelve, she became a sex worker. Not because she wanted to but because her own mother forced her to.

Mackenzie began to live a very normal-looking life by day and a horrific life by night. She hated her life; she wanted out but could not escape—until she heard about JC's Girls and reached out. The ministry was coming to a dramatic close; there was enough finger-pointing and blame to go around. We had all meant well, but it did not end well.

Thank God Mackenzie got hold of one of JC's Girls' true believers, Lori, who felt called to reach women no one else was reaching. Through God's grace, even though the ministry came to an end, Lori kept ministering and developed a relationship with Mackenzie. Over time, Lori developed a sense that Mackenzie sincerely wanted to change.

Changing is not easy for women in the sex industry. One of our greatest challenges as a church was what to do with women who wanted out. We didn't have the training or the finances to truly help these women. Many of them were single moms. They had bills to pay and kids to feed. Some of the sex workers made more money than I did. All we could do was offer low-paying jobs with hesitant companies. It turned out to be very difficult to get wives on board with their husbands hiring women from the sex industry.

Some of the gals would get out of the industry and take part in our church for a while, but the lure of a consistent paycheck was too tempting compared to the long hours and low pay we could help them attain. They needed long-term help. Not days or months but years of help.

My wife and I were in a small group with Lori and her husband, Matt, who one evening brought an idea for us to discuss. They wanted us to pray over whether they should move Mackenzie out of another state to California to live with them. Matt and Lori had two young children, so they wanted our group's spiritual wisdom before moving forward.

No one, including myself, knew what to think about this. At that point, I had never met Mackenzie, so I had no idea what to believe, but I knew what I had observed. Successful sex workers aren't just experienced at sex; they are great at manipulation. They have to be able to convince men that they are into them. The more real the experience feels for the man, the more money for the worker. In my very little time in the ministry, I learned that it was tough to discern who was genuine and who wasn't. I got fooled many times. I don't mean this to sound judgmental; it's just a natural consequence of the industry. These women made their living by pretending they felt certain ways. Being dishonest was normalized, and it was hard for them to be real. After all, being real in their line of work was dangerous.

I wasn't sure about Mackenzie, but Matt and Lori were. So our small group supported them wholeheartedly. A few weeks later, Mackenzie arrived and has been an important part of our lives ever since.

At first, the new family dynamic was hard for Mackenzie. Even the great things were difficult. She had never celebrated a holiday sober. She had never eaten a turkey at Thanksgiving or received a gift from under the tree at Christmas. She had never learned to ride a bike. Mackenzie had a woman's body but seemed so much like a child.

Over time, Mackenzie opened up about the things that happened to her. Some of them are so terrible I can't even write them down. All I can say is, I now know why there is a hell, because if there isn't one for some of the things people did to her, then God is not good.

Mackenzie fit in quickly with Matt and Lori's kids and loved being treated like a little sister by all the wives in the group.

Feeling safe and secure around those of us who were men in the small group was a different story. Mackenzie had been forced into prostitution by her mother, but men did the physical and sexual abuse. Her mother profited, but her torment came from men. Mackenzie had been hurt repeatedly by men who touched her, even men who claimed they were safe. Although I developed a friendship with her, we created a boundary so there was never any physical contact.

Mackenzie lived with our friends for five years, after which she moved in with some gals from our church. Six more years of counseling, six more years of work, and six more years of tears. She has been in a small group with Tammy and me for the past couple of years.

As hard and frustrating as it has been for her, she has

never strayed from her path of healing. She has struggled, and she has sinned, but she has never gone back to the industry. Mackenzie is tough, and she is my hero because she is so open and honest. She still struggles but *never* hides the truth.

I have not always been patient, watching her move so slowly at times—two steps forward and one step back. I've wanted her healing to move on my timeline, but she has been moving on God's. Recently, Mackenzie moved to a new home. She has an incredible job and close friends. To help her move, our small group met at her home, where she was surrounded by men who have proven over the years to be safe and to be men of God. Mackenzie loves to help others but has a hard time receiving help because she is still unsure if she is worthy of love. Receiving help is a part of her healing. And because she is growing, she let us serve her.

We didn't just help her move that day; we celebrated her birthday after unpacking her new place. She is used to cakes and candles now. At first, she hated the attention and all the fuss. But we sang, and she received the love. Tammy and I said our goodbyes, and as we walked out the door Mackenzie reached out and touched my shoulder. When I turned around, she smiled and said, "Thanks." Then she did something she had never done in all these years. She hugged me. I was moved to tears. I knew what it meant for her to reach out to me. Eleven years in the making, that hug was worth the wait. My friend Mackenzie's heart is truly healing.

Over the years in small group, I was not the only one

who was aware of the slow pace of her healing. Mackenzie hated how slow it was too. Healing the heart is never fast; it always takes longer than we would like. So much of what's wrong with us is not a disease but a brokenness. Hospitals are full of hurting people with hearts that look fine from a medical perspective but are broken and bleeding from an emotional one. Just as Mackenzie had to reach out to me to see her next step in the miracle of healing, we all must reach for Jesus if we have a broken heart.

HEALING A BROKEN HEART

In Mark 5, Jesus returned after healing the man with the "Legion" of problems (from chapter 9). The community who witnessed the healing asked Jesus to leave their side of the lake. They were more comfortable with banishing the formerly crazed man than accepting his healing and acknowledging the power of Jesus. The lone witness to the truth of Jesus was the man who had been crazed but was now in his right mind. As Jesus approached the other side of the lake, word of healing spread, and He was welcomed like a celebrity. Everyone wanted to see and touch Jesus.

There, Jesus was met by a wealthy man named Jairus whose twelve-year-old daughter was dying. Jairus begged Jesus to come home with him to heal his only child. Jesus accepted the invitation, but He had to fight through the enormous crowd pressing in on every side. His disciples went from followers to a security team to keep Jesus from being crushed! Everyone wanted a moment with the man of miracles. One woman among the crowd had been suffering from a bleeding disorder for twelve years. Mark's gospel records that she had seen many doctors, who only made her condition worse (v. 26). She was suffering, broke, and alone.

Two thousand years ago, Jewish culture had strict rules for women regarding their menstrual cycles. A woman had to isolate herself during her period. The bed she slept on and the chair she sat on would have been considered unclean. Anyone who came in contact with her would have been unclean. This woman had been bleeding for twelve years, so if she had ever been married her husband would have been long gone. If she had any children, they would not have associated with her. She was all alone in her suffering. Never allowed to touch or to be touched by anyone.

The point of this story is not to judge their culture but to have compassion for this woman's suffering. Don't judge God's heart for the words found in Leviticus from which these laws about menstruation came; but judge God's heart through Jesus. Because He is the Word of God who came and dwelled among us.

The woman in Mark 5 thought that if she could press in and touch Jesus, she would be healed without being discovered. The intense crowd was her cover as she intentionally worked her way through the people, past the disciples, making her way closer to Jesus. The scene was absolute chaos. There was pushing and shoving. While the disciples shouted at the mob to get back, she quietly slipped in, believing she would be healed if her fingertips could touch Jesus' outer clothing.

Over the years, I'm sure this woman had become a master at going unnoticed. Slipping in and out of her village to not arouse any attention. Her only alternative would have been to isolate herself in her home—if she still had one. While she was supposed to be confined to her bed, she made her way into the presence of Jesus. She strained and pressed, but nothing worked. She gave it one last attempt, and then it happened. She touched Him—not really Him, but almost Him. She touched the hem of His clothing! The second she touched Him externally, something instantly changed in her internally. The woman had known the pain of her suffering. It had been an unwelcome foe for over twelve years. And in a second, it was gone. Her healing journey had lasted so long; it was hard and costly. And suddenly, it was over!

The woman didn't even have time to think or celebrate before Jesus turned to the crowd and shouted, "Who touched my garments?" (v. 30).

The disciples were confused. They were all being touched from every angle and by everyone. They said to Jesus, "You see the crowd pressing around you, and yet you say, 'Who touched me?'" (v. 31). Everyone was touching Him!

But Jesus wasn't talking about being touched by everyone. He was concerned only with the touch of someone. This woman, an expert at hiding, had been called out by Jesus. I can almost see Him staring into her eyes as He asked, "Who touched my garments?" Jesus knew they had made a connection. And she knew He meant her. He had felt His power leave Him. And she had felt His power heal her.

If she answered honestly, she could be hurt by the crowd. In her condition she wasn't supposed to come into contact with *anyone*, much less intentionally reach out and touch a holy man! The woman was terrified, but she'd been caught. She went from being overwhelmed by her miracle to being terrified by her fate as a law-breaker. She fell to her knees and confessed her action. Jesus, the perfect image of God, did not judge her; instead He blessed her.

Jesus did not come to judge you but to heal you. Inside and out, just like He healed this woman. As she trembled at his feet, Jesus turned to her and said, "Daughter, your faith has made you well; go in peace, and be healed of your disease" (v. 34).

You can probably guess by now which Greek word is translated as "well" in this verse. It's *sozo*. It's what Jesus does because it's who He is. If your heart is broken and needs healing, there is so much for you to learn in this story.

Don't Let Broken People Keep You from Jesus

The first thing to learn is that no matter who breaks your heart, don't let them keep you from Jesus. The church is full of broken people. Sometimes it even has evil people. I am sorry for whatever these people did to you. Remember, it wasn't God, and it wasn't His church that hurt you. It was a person or a group of people. The woman in Mark 5 didn't let the crowds keep her from Jesus, and you shouldn't either.

Some of my best life experiences have come through church life. Still, my church experience hasn't been perfect.

Some of my deepest wounds have come from Christians. When I was a child, there was a youth volunteer at my church who many considered handsome, talented, and charming. But he had a dark side. He was angry and could, without notice, become violent. I had heard of it happening to others in our group, but I was shocked when it happened to me.

We were out of town at a youth conference playing flag football in the hotel's parking lot. We had divided into two teams. I was on one, and this man was on the other. I don't know exactly what I said, but it set him off big-time. Now, if you've heard or seen me preach, you know my mouth is much bigger than my body. My mouth has always been a blessing and a burden. Well, it must have been working overtime that day, and this guy snapped.

All of a sudden he hit me, and I hit the ground. I remember waking up and hearing kids crying. This guy was on top of me, and his hands were around my neck choking me. People were screaming for him to stop. Eventually, some of the larger boys in the group pulled him off, and he ran away screaming.

What do you do when those who are supposed to protect you are the ones that hurt you?

All night long, my friends and I huddled in our hotel room in fear. This was before cell phones, so we didn't know what to do. At some point, the guy knocked on our door. His eyes were still wild, and he was clearly still angry. We didn't want to let him in, but we did. He told us that if we said anything about what he did in the parking lot, he would be in big trouble and might even kill himself. First I had been abused, and now I was being manipulated—by a "man of God."

I blamed God that night, and then I spent the next few years running from Him, making a total mess of my life.

Years later, while I was in college, my mom sent me a package I had to pick up. When I arrived at The UPS Store, the man working at the counter was a little scary and a total jerk. I was a little older but not any smarter. The guy yelled at me, "Do you want your package or what?" With a bit of attitude, I replied, "Of course," grabbed my package, and stormed out to my car.

Sitting in my car, I realized the man working at UPS reminded me of the man who had hurt me years earlier. I heard God say, *Do you want* Me *or not?* I said, "Of course." The Holy Spirit said, *Then don't blame Me for people who wear My uniform.* I realized I had been blaming God for someone who wanted to appear to be His follower but didn't live like one. I had let my church hurt get in the way of my relationship with Jesus. Nothing, not even your pain, is more important than your relationship with God.

Don't Let Past Hurts and Failures Get in the Way

The bleeding woman who touched Jesus' hem didn't let her past hurts and failures get in the way of reaching out for Jesus. She pressed through many of the people in her community who had wounded her. As you may have noticed, this story didn't begin with her. The bleeding woman's miracle fell in the middle of another story.

A rich and religiously powerful man was worried about his twelve-year-old daughter dying. The first words the woman who had been suffering for twelve years with a bleeding disorder heard when she confessed to being the one who touched Jesus was—wait for it—"Daughter" (v. 34). Your parents on earth may not be rich or power-ful, but your Father in heaven is. Your parents on earth may not have loved you, but your Father in heaven does! The twelve years allude to the fact the Jesus loves us all equally! The first step to your healing is recognizing that you are not what people did to hurt you; you are a son or daughter of the King of kings, and that's why Jesus died for you.

Part of your healing journey is knowing your worth! You may feel worthless, but God thought you were worth Christ!

Share Your Story

The next step in your healing journey is *crucial*. Jesus could have allowed this woman to be healed in silence. The miracle had already happened. Why didn't Jesus let her go? Jesus didn't need the attention or glory. As a matter of fact, He often told people to be quiet about the miracle they received. So why did Jesus call her out?

The answer is that for her to be *completely* healed she needed to share her story. So often, as we saw Him do with the man healed from Legion, Jesus sent healed people back to their communities to tell their story.

This woman would not have had the courage to do it herself. Isn't it interesting that she had more faith to pur-sue a miracle than she had to be exposed when the miracle worked? Jesus exposed her not to embarrass her but to truly release her. That's why some of His last words to her were, "Go in peace" (v. 34).

By telling your story, you can become stronger and complete your miraculous healing. It is always scary to tell people what happened. I tell our church often, "If you want to heal, you have got to learn to be real." You don't have to tell *everyone everything*. But you do need to learn to tell *someone something* if you want to experience true and lasting healing. Especially if it is a wound of the heart!

Reach for Others to Help You

I realize that your emotional wounds have come at the hands of others. Some of those people who hurt you may have been religious people in positions of power. The woman who bled for twelve years didn't have to overcome a person or a group of people who had hurt her but an entire culture and religious community. She was all alone, and then she reached for Jesus. As you reach for Jesus, know He may ask you to reach for others to complete your miracle.

My friend Mackenzie could have given up on people. Based on her continued experience, she could have assumed that no one was safe and there were no good men in the world. But she didn't give up. She pushed through the crowd and reached out for Jesus by reaching out to His church. Sandals Church is not perfect, but it is full of people who worship a perfect Jesus.

In your own church, Jesus may want you, like Mackenzie, to reach out to His imperfect followers to help bring healing to your life. I don't know whether Mackenzie would have been healed if she hadn't connected with my dear friends

Matt and Lori, who opened their home so Jesus could heal Mackenzie's heart.

If you are hurting and need an emotional miracle, Jesus may borrow someone else's hands to help Him heal your heart wounds. The devil may have used a person to hurt you, but the Lord can use people to help you. I am praying that you will reach out again. Don't give up on Him or His church. These are hands He still uses to heal!

PRAY

Lord Jesus, it's hard for me to trust. I have been hurt so many times. Like the bleeding woman who was all out of money, I am almost all out of hope. Give me the strength to reach again. Help me find the church community to help me heal my broken heart! I pray this in Your name, amen.

WATCH

REFLECT

1. Why do you think it takes so long to heal the human heart?
2. Are there areas of your heart that may still need to be healed?
3. What can you do to have more patience with those who have had their heart broken?
4. How can you work to be a person of trust for those who have been hurt?
5. How can you open up your life to helping someone on a long healing journey?

TWELVE

JESUS CAN DO MIRACLES THROUGH YOU

> "I TELL YOU THE TRUTH. ANYONE WHO BELIEVES IN ME WILL DO THE SAME WORKS I HAVE DONE. AND EVEN GREATER WORKS."
>
> JOHN 14:12 NLT

So many people who believe in Jesus never share the healing power of Jesus. We need to change that. People don't just need Jesus for eternity—they need Him now.

Often, we think of hell as something off in the distance, but for far too many people, it is very real in the present. For the hurting, it is here and now.

As Christians, we are not just called to share His message but to share His healing in our communities. We might not feel like we are ever supposed to offer healing, but the earliest Christians would disagree. The Bible is full of stories of when God used people beyond their abilities. This is what God does! This is what Jesus wants His disciples to do!

It couldn't be any clearer that the disciples of Jesus are supposed to help heal a hurting world than in the Gospel of Luke. Jesus sent His disciples out with this message:

> He sent them out to proclaim the kingdom of God and to heal. (9:2)

Most Christians hear the first part but miss the second. As Christians, we have two missions. First, we are to tell the world about the saving power of Jesus. This is proclaiming the kingdom of God. Second, we are to demonstrate His power through miraculous healings. Jesus did not tell His disciples to do one or the other but to do both.

When Christians hear a message in Scripture, they often only obey part of its commandment. At times, we intentionally pretend to be ignorant. At other times, we miss the clear meaning of the commands of Scripture. We are human; it happens. Jesus wants us to obey all of His commands.

"THE HARVEST IS PLENTIFUL, BUT THE LABORERS ARE FEW"

If you have been in church long enough, you have heard a sermon about the disparity between the spiritual harvest and the number of workers. Jesus said, "The harvest is plentiful, but the laborers are few; therefore pray earnestly to the Lord of the harvest to send out laborers into his harvest" (Matthew 9:37–38).

Most Christians agree with Jesus that we need more laborers, but what kinds of laborers are few? In Scripture, context always matters. Most of us have probably read these verses and felt convicted on some level to serve God more. If you haven't, you should.

As a pastor, I can tell you that your local church is always in need of more people willing to be laborers. The church is full of way too many would-be influencers and not enough people under the influence of the Holy Spirit! The church needs people who are willing to serve in kids' ministry. In counseling. As an usher or greeter. Sometimes this text in Matthew is used more radically to call for someone to become a different kind of laborer, like a missionary or surrendering to "full-time" ministry. That last one cracks me up because I have never found a verse in the Bible where God is looking for "part-time" disciples—even though our churches seem to be full of them.

But what we miss in these verses is not that God is looking for laborers. We miss what kind of laborers are needed.

Before we move forward with these verses, we need to take a step back to understand why Jesus said this. The famous portion of this teaching is found in Matthew 9:37–38. But we must visit the preceding verses to understand why Jesus said it and how to move forward as the kind of laborer God wants. Fortunately, all we have to do is go back a few verses to see exactly why Jesus said we should pray for more laborers.

Just two verses earlier in Matthew 9, we read:

> And Jesus went throughout all the cities and villages, teaching in their synagogues and proclaiming the gospel of the kingdom and healing every disease and every affliction. (v. 35)

In this verse, Jesus was clearly doing two things: He was proclaiming the gospel and *healing* people!

Then the text says that He was moved with compassion. Not just for people who were headed to hell but for people who were hurting on earth. Jesus saw that the people were "harassed and helpless" (v. 36). When Jesus looks at the earth, He does not see a world that needs to be judged. The world is already under judgment; that's why it's so broken. He saw broken people who needed healing.

Jesus calls those hurting, helpless, broken people "sheep without a shepherd" (v. 36). All these sheep need a shepherd who will save and heal them. In the eyes of Jesus, there are plenty of broken, hurting people in this world who are ready for a change! Jesus said there are more people who are ready to be helped than those who are ready to help them. Then Jesus called His disciples to pray, not just for laborers but for people who will work hard to help those who need it the most.

Jesus is calling you and me to love the people in this world with His love that saves *and* heals! Historically, the church has never been more hurtful than when it has forgotten its mission to bring healing. After Jesus said, "The harvest is plentiful, but the laborers are few," and that we should "pray earnestly to the Lord of the harvest to send out laborers" (vv. 37–38), He then turned to His disciples and "gave them authority over unclean spirits, to cast them out, and to heal every disease and every affliction" (10:1).

This is why so many churches are failing today. We proclaim only the gospel. The gospel without the healing power of Jesus is just religious noise in our culture. Your community doesn't care how much noise you make until you can offer something for their pain. So many churches have grandiose mission statements, often about how many lost people they want to reach. There is nothing wrong with wanting to reach lost people. I have spent the last twenty-five years trying to reach the lost.

But according to Jesus, the best way to help those who are lost is to start by helping them with their pain.

JESUS STILL DOES MIRACLES

When I started Sandals Church, I was one of those pastors with grandiose ideas and visions. If I could go back and do it again, I would focus on healing and helping people before I tried to save them. I am not saying you should not share the gospel. In my experience, people are ready to hear the good news when they see it in the form of a healing miracle or a need that is met. We tend to believe in the kingdom of God when we experience its reality in our lives.

I have heard pastors say Jesus no longer does miracles like we see in the Bible. I can tell you this: no matter how well-meaning they are or how much they know about the Scriptures, Jesus still heals, still helps, and on occasion still raises the dead. I know; I have personally seen it.

In the summer of 2012, I had to change the way I viewed the healing power of Jesus. I had seen miracles before, but what I needed on this occasion was a Lazarus-like miracle. If you don't know who Lazarus was, John 11 tells us that he was a close friend of Jesus and that he had died. Then Jesus miraculously brought him back to life. This was precisely the kind of miracle I needed.

My family and I went on a medical mission trip to Northern Vietnam. The land was beautiful, and the people were warm and wonderful. Vietnam was a scary place for my parents' generation. For them it was a land of war, pain, and death. For me it will forever be the place where I saw Jesus heal. Our medical missionaries performed surgeries at no cost to people in desperate need of a medical miracle. Everything was warm and wonderful—until it wasn't.

I am not a medical professional. I was the mission's chaplain and served primarily as a pastor for our medical team. I have no medical training, so I spent my days encouraging staff and meeting with potential candidates for surgery. After a long day in the fields of Northern Vietnam, I returned to base camp. "We have a problem," one of the doctors informed me with panic in his voice. The medical team had performed cleft palate surgery on a young boy, and the boy was having major complications coming out of anesthesia. The doctor asked if I would accompany him to the hospital. I thought it was a strange request because I had no medical training whatsoever, but I went with him without mentioning my confusion.

When I arrived at the hospital, I was greeted by more doctors from our team. They shared that the situation was dire. The boy was not breathing. They asked me to scrub in so I could pray over the young boy. I was overwhelmed. After all, we had state-of-the-art technology on our trip and some of the best medical doctors. When you're not breathing, you should go to the doctor or hospital, not to your pastor.

After vigorously scrubbing my hands and putting on a surgical gown, I was quickly escorted through the hospital's surgical wing. Things felt normal until I turned a corner and was instantly immersed in the chaos. There was shouting and screaming. Fingers were pointing, people were pacing, and it seemed like everyone was yelling in different directions.

One huge doctor from Texas grabbed a metal surgical dish, threw the pan with great force against the wall, and screamed, "The boy is dead! Just call it!"

Those were the first words I heard clearly as I turned and saw a young boy lying lifeless on the surgical table. He was so tiny, so blue, so naked, and even to me so obviously dead. At that moment, I vividly remembered having been

quickly rushed past a crying Vietnamese family in the hallway. I recalled the mother looking straight into my soul, her
fear-filled eyes silently pleading for help.

I snapped back to reality as the head doctor of our mission, Dr. Vien Doan, looked me square in the eye and said,
"I am not calling it until after you pray over the boy."

I looked at him in complete shock. "Until after I pray?"

"Yes, Pastor. Please pray."

I cannot fully express what I experienced at that
moment because I don't have the words to describe what
I felt. Whenever you meet or feel the spiritual world, you
cannot compare it with anything physical from this world.
The only thing I can do to describe what I felt would be to
use the word *weight*. Extreme, crushing weight all around
me. I felt like this weight was pressing my entire body into
the earth and beyond. I had never felt anything as heavy
as this. The thickness was all around me. It was on me. I
wanted to run but could not move.

The room, which had been filled with screaming when
I walked in, became silent. I looked around the room full
of doctors, nurses, an anesthesiologist, his assistant, the
surgeon who had performed the surgery, and a handful of
interpreters. They were all staring at me. I looked down at
the boy, then at Dr. Doan, and said, "Let's pray."

The medical team began to head out of the room, and
in a panicked voice I asked them where they were going.
We were all in this together. Right then and there, I had the
entire team hold hands like we were children, and I began
to pray. I don't remember everything I said, but I remember
these words:

Lord, we came here to help, but we hurt this boy. We wanted to improve his life, but I am afraid we took it . . .

I placed my hands on the little guy's lifeless body and began crying to God. I have no idea how long I prayed; time seemed to stand still, but I know that I was scared to death to say amen. I gave my prayer a zero percent chance of success. In my Baptist circles I had never even heard of someone being raised from the dead. In my tradition, we prayed up until death; if you died, that was God's answer. But this time, I prayed that the Lord Jesus would heal this lifeless body.

I didn't know that the issue and the attempt to revive the boy had gone on for hours. That's why the doctor who threw the pan was so angry. All the doctors knew the boy was gone, everyone but Dr. Doan. I prayed, cried, and screamed, "God, heal him in Jesus' name!" Then, with almost no faith at all, I said amen. I opened my eyes and looked at the lifeless body. The room was silent. The boy was still. My hands were on his cold chest.

Then I felt something move.

I looked to my left, and the little guy's penis rose straight up! Not a resurrection but an erection for sure! Then he peed. I mean, he peed a *lot*. They had been pumping his body full of fluids for hours, and it came out! I stepped back in shock and looked at the boy's face. His eyes opened. He stared straight at me. The doctor scooped him up into his arms.

And the room broke out in collective praise.

Tears of joy streamed down the surgeon's face. He put

his hand on my shoulder. "It's a miracle," he said, "just like in the Bible!"

The boy was healed within seconds of the words "in Jesus' name, amen"! They ran all kinds of tests, but he was perfectly fine. Within the hour, the little guy was in his mother's arms. He had not been breathing for eight hours. And yet he had no brain damage and is still, to this day, miraculously, completely healed!

WHY IS IT SO HARD FOR US TO BELIEVE?

I recently preached at one of the largest, most successful churches of our time. I shared this exact story. The auditorium was full of thousands of dedicated believers. They had been discipled by one of the best preachers of our age. But they sat there staring at me when I told them this story. They probably thought what some of you are thinking. *Really? Did that happen? Could that happen?*

Isn't it interesting that to be a Christian, you must believe that people can come back from the dead? Because if they can't, then what do we do with a dead Jesus?

Why is it so hard for us to believe that the risen Son of God, who defeated death Himself, could not do it for someone else? Why have we, as Christians, become so hard-hearted when it comes to dynamic miracles like these? I didn't claim I did it; I claimed Jesus did it!

I knew this church would struggle with the miracle I

was proclaiming. Heck, I'm struggling writing this, and I was there, right there, when it happened. So I invited a special guest with me that day.

I stood onstage at Saddleback Church in sunny Southern California and asked Dr. Vien Doan, who was sitting in the front row, if what I was saying was true. If the boy came to life, would he please stand and shout out loud that every word I shared about this was true. So he did, and the place erupted. People were standing, people were cheering, and people were reminded that Jesus still heals!

Jesus has not sent you just to tell people about Jesus. He has sent you to share the healing power of heaven! When Jesus sent the disciples out, He sent them to proclaim the gospel and to heal (Matthew 9:37–10:1). I encourage you to reread the Gospels and look at all the healing that takes place. Healing helps the hurting with believing. It helps the world trust God so they can be healed from the inside out!

HE IS STILL THE SAME JESUS

You and I may not be able to do the same miracles as Jesus. But He can still do the same miracles because He is still the same Jesus.

We need to do everything in our power to bring people before His power. We need the healing power of Jesus now more than ever. For too long, Christians have settled for personal power, political power, and many other forms of power that are destructive to themselves and the world. The only power we should seek is the healing power of Jesus.

I brought Dr. Doan with me that day as a witness to the healing power of Jesus, to remind Saddleback Church of the same thing I am reminding you. The Bible testifies not only to the miracles of Jesus but to the eyewitnesses of those miracles who in turn testify to the healing power of Jesus. The Scriptures are full of people like me and Dr. Doan who saw a miracle with our own eyes. Jesus heals!

Christianity is not just a life insurance policy for eternity—it is a health insurance plan for life on earth. Jesus is the Great Physician, and as the Great Physician, He came for those who are sick and need healing.

> Jesus answered them, "Healthy people don't need a doctor—sick people do. I have come to call not those who think they are righteous, but those who know they are sinners and need to repent." (Luke 5:31–32 NLT)

Jesus loves you. Jesus has saved you. Now Jesus wants to use you to bring healing to someone else. I know it's scary. The things of God often are, but with Jesus you can do all things!

HOW TO BE USED BY JESUS FOR MIRACLES

To be used by Jesus for something miraculous, you need to do a couple of things.

Confess Your Lack of Faith

The first is to simply confess your lack of faith in this area. Every believer has this struggle; therefore, you should be willing to confess this sin. We are all of "little faith" (Matthew 8:26).

As I approached this young boy lying dead on the table, I knew there was nothing I could do. When we pray for a miracle, there is nothing that we can do. As Christians, we tend to get wrapped up in everything but our faith in God.

As I walked into the hospital, I entered a realm beyond my expertise. I knew I was beyond my level of intelligence and wisdom. But Dr. Doan wasn't looking for wisdom or intelligence; he was looking for *faith*. As a doctor, he focused on this young child's medical care. He'd turned to me, assuming that I would be focused on spiritual care. I want to be clear—at that moment, I was not a man of great faith. I was a man of extraordinarily small faith. I was just as shocked at the miracle as every medical professional in the room. Still, in that moment I realized my role as a person of faith. Just as the medical staff was trained to save lives, I needed to train myself to pray in faith to God even in the face of death.

Over the years, I have worked with first responders, doctors, nurses, policemen, firemen, and ambulance personnel. These are incredibly stressful jobs. These men and women are all trained to keep their wits about them and do their job when someone's life is on the line. As Christians, we are all first responders and must train ourselves to respond in faith.

As believers, we must not run *from* these emergencies but *to* them. Not because you or I can do anything, but because we pray to Jesus, God's one and only Son, who can do all things.

My lack of faith came from being sinfully focused on myself. I am not asking you to believe in magic, and I have no idea what God will do when you pray. But I am asking you to believe in what the Messiah *can* do. Jesus said, "For nothing will be impossible with God" (Luke 1:37). He meant *nothing*. No matter how terrible a situation is, we can and should still pray.

Jesus faced these situations, and you will too. You can't choose whether or not they happen, but you can choose to be ready. Even Jesus got ready. Before Jesus died on the cross and rose from the dead, He readied Himself. Every miracle Jesus performed built upon another. The Bible says, "Jesus grew in wisdom and in stature and in favor with God and all the people" (Luke 2:52 NLT). If Jesus grew, so should you! In the Gospel of John, Jesus' first miracle was new wine, and His last miracle was the new covenant, proven by His resurrection. But before Jesus rose Himself, He raised his friend Lazarus.

Lazarus had been dead four days, one day longer than Jesus would be. But Jesus did not run from death; He went straight to the grave of Lazarus. In His years on earth, growing in wisdom and with God, Jesus chose to be ready. He called forth Lazarus, and Lazarus came back to life.

You may never see a miracle like this. I still can't believe God allowed me to see one. But in this story, you and I are not Jesus, and if you are reading this, you are not Lazarus. But we are always Martha.

Jesus made an incredible statement and then asked Martha, the living sister of the dead Lazarus, a powerful question:

> Jesus told her, "I am the resurrection and the life. Anyone who believes in me will live, even after dying. Everyone who lives in me and believes in me will never ever die. Do you believe this, Martha?" (John 11:25–26 NLT)

We all must ask this question when we pray for miracles: Do you believe that Jesus is the resurrection and the life? If we do believe this, we can pray in faith even in the face of death. Martha's response was the same as almost every believer's: "Yes, Lord, I believe." She actually went one step further and said, "I have always believed" (v. 27 NLT). We often assume we have faith leading to eternal life until we are faced with death in the here and now!

Martha believed that she had a complete and very real faith until Jesus did something that exposed her lack of faith. Jesus loved Martha, but He was frustrated by her lack of faith. She believed she had the needed faith; Jesus showed her the faith she still lacked.

Jesus approached the tomb of Lazarus and said, "Roll the stone aside" (v. 39 NLT). Then Martha, who said she had always believed, tried to stop a miracle of Jesus!

> But Martha, the dead man's sister, protested, "Lord, he has been dead for four days. The smell will be terrible." (v. 39 NLT)

Martha, a woman of faith, was still focused on the physical world. I wonder how many times we have stopped a miracle of Jesus because we were more concerned with the mess a prayer of faith would make as opposed to the stench of our lack of faith in God. The good news is that Jesus went ahead and prayed for a miracle anyway.

> Jesus looked up to heaven and said, "Father, thank you for hearing me. You always hear me, but I said it out loud for the sake of all these people standing here, so that they will believe you sent me." Then Jesus shouted, "Lazarus, come out!" (vv. 41–43 NLT)

Jesus prayed, Lazarus rose, and the world changed. Someone was dead, but he was miraculously brought back to life. This was an amazing miracle, and miracles like this can still happen. But they won't happen if we don't pray.

Pray

The second thing you must do to be used by Jesus for miracles is pray; there is *no* other way. Jesus prayed to God out loud. He did this for you, and He did this for me. He said, "I said it out loud for the sake of all these people standing here." But ultimately, Jesus didn't only do this miracle for the people standing around but for all those who have heard this story and His prayer. Jesus prayed out loud to show us how to connect with God when we need Him the most. We need to pray *out loud*.

So many of us Christians talk about prayer, but so many fail to actually pray. While finishing this book, I was reminded once again of the power of a spoken prayer. What I mean by that is when prayers are *actually* prayed. Many times, rather than pray, we say that we are sending our thoughts and prayers. I think people should keep their thoughts to themselves. If you ever feel led to pray for me, you can keep your thoughts, but by all means, send your prayers!

But how do we send our prayers? You don't send them to me. You send them to God by praying your prayers. We have to stop hashtagging #prayer and start actually praying like Jesus did. Stop worrying, stop sending thoughts, and start sending your prayers to God!

As I was writing this, the entire NFL and sports worlds were shocked to watch one of its players lie lifelessly on the field. I watched the strongest, toughest men weep on the field. In an instant, they went from men with godlike strength to men with childlike fear.

That's what death does. It shakes even the bravest of us. The game no longer mattered, and the team they played for no longer mattered; the playoffs no longer mattered. All that mattered was Damar. Everyone watched as the team doctors worked on Damar Hamlin, who played safety for the Buffalo Bills.

Damar had been struck in the chest as he tackled an opposing player. He'd popped up like nothing was wrong and then immediately fell to the ground again because his heart stopped beating.

The longer the team doctors worked, the bleaker the outcome looked. The game was canceled, and the fans went home. But many would never be the same. It was horrifying to watch.

The internet was ablaze with #prayfordamar. Prayers and well wishes poured in from everywhere. Yet Damar still struggled, and his future continued to look grim. Then I saw something I had never seen. A sports announcer, moved by emotion and concern, did something on national TV we all should do. He did what Jesus did. He didn't talk about prayer; he actually prayed! He said he believed in prayer, and he believed in God. He said he wasn't going to talk about prayer; he was *going* to pray. It was awesome. He put his faith over his future career and asked God for a miracle.

Against all odds, Damar Hamlin is alive today. It was reported that his first question after coming out of his coma was, "Who won the game?" The doctors reportedly answered, "You did, Damar; you won the game of life."

We will never know what would have happened if people had not prayed. The doctors did their best—but in this case, so did the believers.

How many miracles might you see if you started praying out loud, wherever you are, whenever you need a miracle? Jesus needed one, and He said, "Father, thank you for hearing me. You always hear me" (John 11:41–42 NLT).

> **I have often wondered if God might someday show us all the yeses we didn't get because we didn't ask.**

We don't know what God will do when we ask for miracles, but we know that God will always listen. We don't have to believe that He *will* do a miracle. We just have to believe that He can!

I have often wondered if God might someday show us all the yeses we didn't get because we didn't ask.

Your job is to pray. God's job is to answer. Don't leave this life with miracles in heaven sitting on the shelf.

Every day there is an opportunity for a miracle. As you go through this life, look for those who might need prayer. People all around you need miracles. They need a miracle to pay rent, a miracle for their loved one battling addiction. They need a miracle to stay married. They might even need a miracle to stay alive. You and I are not miracle workers, but we love and follow the One who is.

———

Thank you so much for reading this book. I hope that from this day forward you will never again doubt what God can do but rather pray to Him because of what you believe He can do!

If you enjoyed this book, you can start praying about who God would have you share it with. Maybe God will start His miracle in their lives by using you to share this book and open their eyes to the Miracle Worker. The Healer, His name is Jesus.

PRAY

Lord Jesus, please move powerfully in my life. I want to see You do miracles. If it is Your will, please give me the faith to allow You to do miracles through me and the courage to begin to pray for healing in the lives of hurting people. In Your name I pray, amen.

WATCH

REFLECT

1. How could God use you to do something miraculous in your life?
2. How can you look for opportunities to pray for God's healing power in the lives of those around you?
3. Where do you need to personally grow in your faith journey to allow God to do more through you?
4. How can you start praying for miracles right now?
5. When you see God do something miraculous, how can you work on sharing His wonders and telling your friends about Jesus?

ACKNOWLEDGMENTS

I would like to thank everyone at W Publishing and HarperCollins who worked so hard to help me tell this story—specifically Kyle Olund, who helped to maintain my voice through the editing process. He always is encouraging, and without him, this book never would have come to life.

Next, my thanks to Lori Zimbardi. I could never be a writer without you. You gave me the courage to throw away my first attempt at this book and led me to its current format. Thank you for your constant encouragement and long hours helping during this difficult process. You were my cheerleader when I wanted to quit!

To Jennifer, you saw this book from its beginning. What I loved most about your feedback was all the "wows"! When I first saw the almost one hundred comments to work through, I was nervous. So many of them were encouraging. Especially when you took time to tell me you laughed or were moved personally!

To Kit, we are strangers, but your words helped make my words better. Thank you for what you do. I loved your feedback and your suggestions! Thank you for doing your best when my writing was at its worst!

To Brooke, thank you for helping me get this book to the finish line! When I was out of energy and creativity you gave me exactly what I needed! Your attention to detail caught so many things I had missed. Your clarifying thoughts were powerful and will help to bring the reader along when I was vague and confusing! The exclamation point was for you! You know how I love them!!!!

To Damon, who first said no to this project! Thank you for giving me a chance to tell some of the most amazing miracles that I have seen Jesus do over the years.

To all the brave and courageous people who allowed me to share their personal stories to bring hope to the hopeless and healing to the broken—thank you.

ABOUT THE AUTHOR

Matthew Stephen Brown is the founding and lead pastor of Sandals Church in Riverside, California. Sandals Church began in 1997 when Pastor Matt and his wife, Tammy, set out to create a church where people could be real with themselves, God, and others. From its first meeting in the Browns' living room with eight people, Sandals Church has grown to include fourteen physical campuses throughout California.

In addition, Sandals Church has a growing online campus, with people from sixty-three countries tuning in to hear the sermon each week, as well as a podcast called *The Debrief with Matthew Stephen Brown*, where Pastor Matt tackles biblical truths and cultural issues in an informative and humorous way.

Today, Pastor Matt continues to lead Sandals Church as the primary teaching pastor. And in 2019, Sandals Church launched the ROGO Foundation, which exists to help save and replant dying churches and invest in up-and-coming leaders through hands-on leadership training programs at

Sandals Church. Pastor Matt is passionate about the vision of authenticity and raising up the next generation of leaders for the local church.

He and Tammy have three children and reside in Riverside, California.